Waldemar Góralski, Dariusz Miszczak

The Japanese Cruiser Maya

I0883318

KAGERO

Portside.

Following the defeat in the Guadalcanal campaign, at the beginning of 1943, the Navy Technical Department and The High Command of the Imperial Japanese Navy strived to increase the defensive potential of all their warships. Apart from standard refits of the majority of the Imperial Japanese Navy units, a plan was adopted, which called for reconstruction of two "Takao" class heavy cruisers into anti-aircraft units. Through a coincidence only the Maya underwent such conversion. This publication shows the cruiser in her anti-aircraft configuration and briefly describes her career.

In March 1927, the Japanese government appropriated the budget of 261.31 million yen (in 1928, the rate of exchange was $1=2.3 yen) for the five-year New Warship-Building Replenishment Program, which called for construction of 27 warships. Within the allocated funds, the amount of 113.48 million yen would be spent on construction of four heavy cruisers of a new class (A-class). These ships would be built in compliance with the limitations of the Washington Treaty signed in 1922. The units, with displacement of 10.000 t (long ton=Imperial ton=1016.05 kg), were an improved version of the previous "Myōkō" class design. They were assigned provisional designations from No.9 to No.12. However, according to plan, the construction of the first two vessels would begin in 1927, with the other pair to follow the next year. On September 11, 1928, vessel No.11 was given the name *Maya* after the mountain located in the vicinity of the city where her construction would commence. The keel was finally laid down on December 11, 1928, in a private shipyard of the Kawasaki Dockyard Company Ltd. in Kobe. It was eight months behind schedule due to the bankruptcy of the company. The construction began with the endorsement and protection of the Navy. The ceremonial launching took place on November 8, 1930, and was attended by a crowd of 30 thousand spectators. The fitting-out work followed. On April 4, 1932, during a speed trial in the Kii Strait (separating the islands of Honshu and Shikoku), the ship attained the maximum speed of 35 knots, with the displacement of 12.175 t.

Operational history

Period before the outbreak of World War II

The cruiser was accepted by a naval commission on June 30, 1932, and registered at the Yokosuka Naval Station. She was maintained as the first reserve ship, so that her crew would undergo training. On December 1, 1932, all four "Takao" class units were assigned to the 4th Cruiser Division (Sentai 4) of the Second Fleet (Kantai 2) as replacement of the "Myōkō" class cruisers. In 1933, ships of the Squadron participated in gunnery exercises, took part in Special Great Manoeuvres and in the Naval Review off Yokohama. On September 12, cruiser *Maya* was dry-docked at Yokosuka. During the overhaul, the wireless equipment was replaced, new secondary battery directors were mounted and improvements were made to the main battery command installation. Huge air intakes were installed in the rear section of the bridge tower. The work on the 4th Squadron vessels was completed on February 2, 1934, and on the same day they left Tokyo Bay, heading for the area off Kyushu for a two-month training. By the end of October, the Squadron returned to Yokosuka for refitting. Their steering gear installation was improved, which in the case of the *Maya* lasted from October 22 until December 20. At that time the ship received, a new, three-seat Kawanishi E7K1 "Alf" reconnaissance floatplane. In March-April, 1935, the Squadron operated in the waters of the East China Sea. In August-September, the 4th Cruiser Squadron again participated in Great Manoeuvres. On December 1, the *Maya* and the *Takao* were again assigned to the 4th Cruiser Squadron of the Second Fleet, and the former became the Squadron's flagship. The ship received new, two-seat Nakajima E8N1 "Dave" reconnaissance floatplanes, which replaced the E4N2 ones. In the period between March 27 and April 6, 1937, both cruisers left Sasebo and, as part of a routine training, headed for mainland China. Due to the fighting in Shanghai, since August 20, the cruiser *Maya*, along with the 5th Cruiser Squadron and lighter units took part in the redeployment of the troops from Nagoya to Chusan Islands (at present Zhoushan, China). Between December 8, 1937, and January 14, 1938, the *Maya* was slightly modified at Yokosuka. Her donkey boiler installation was replaced, cruising modification on four shafts was adopted, the foremast was shortened, searchlights replaced by new, stronger ones and light anti-aircraft artillery was replaced. Both *Chōkai* and *Maya* were scheduled to undergo a similar refit as their sister ships from January 1941. However, since the preparations for war had already begun and the ships had to be ready in June 1941, the modernization program for them was cancelled on November 15, 1940. Between March 11-28, the ships participated in warlike manoeuvres off southern Kyushu and returned to Yokosuka on March 30. All the units of the Division were dry-docked; in the case of *Maya*, this took place from April 2 until 10, at the Yokohama shipyard. It is possible, that following the refit, the cruiser, similarly to other units of the class, took part in manoeuvres, sailing around Kyushu and Shikoku. *Maya* was again dry-docked, between September 2 and 9, at Kure, where she was stationed with *Chōkai*, being prepared for war. The characteristic degaussing cables may have been installed on both

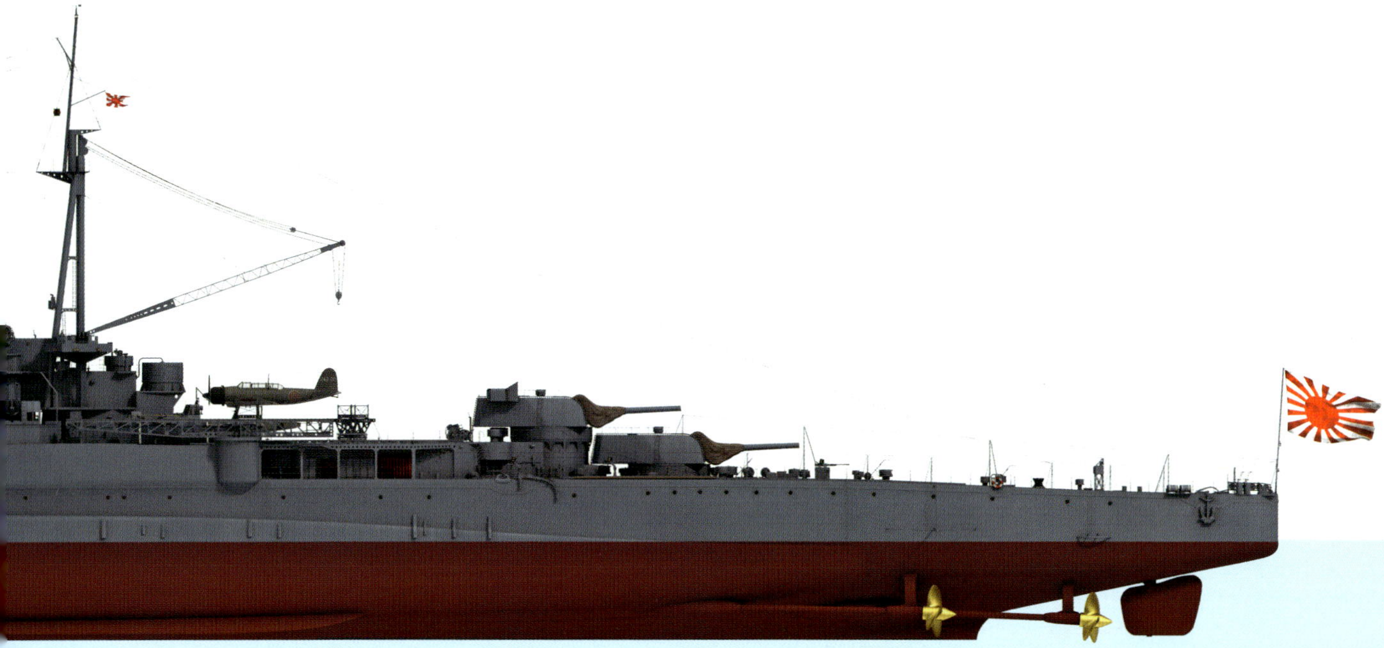

units at that time. On November 5, final war preparations had begun and the ships started loading stores, fuel and ammunition. Then they sailed to their respective staging bases. The cruiser *Maya*, prepared for war, was at Hashirajima anchorage in Kure, awaiting orders. On November 12, she was joined by her sister ship *Atago* and on November 25, both units steamed to Saeki, arriving there on November 27. They were joined by the cruiser *Takao*. Two days later, the ships left the bay and headed for Mako, where they arrived on December 2. On that day, commander of the Second Fleet, Vice Admiral Nobutake Kondō, who became the commander of the South Area Force, hoisted his flag on the *Takao*. While stationed there, the ships received the order, transmitted from the high command of the Combined Fleet, which set the date of the attack against the Allied forces on December 8 (Japan time). The objective of the South Area Force was to reinforce and secure the invasion of Malaya and the Philippines (M and L Operations). The cruiser *Maya* was attached to the main force, however, on December 4, the cruiser detached and headed back to Mako. Three days later, she joined Vice Admiral Ibō Takahashi's Third Fleet, the Philippine Seizure Force.

The war, December 1941 to July 1942

The cruiser *Maya* left the Pescadores on December 7 with a portion of the Japanese forces and covered the landings at Aparri and Vigan in northern Philippines on December 10-11. In the morning of December 10, west of Luzon, the ships were attacked by five Consolidated PBY-4 Catalina flying boats. U.S. planes scored no hits. *Maya* returned to Mako on December 14 and five days later, with units of the Philippine Seizure Force, she escorted the convoy and on December 22, supported the landing in the Lingayen Gulf. She returned to the Pescadores the next day. The ship put to sea again on December 31, to cover the Third Malaya Convoy. She returned to base on January 4, 1942. On January 18, *Maya* joined Vice Admiral Nobutake Kondō's forces and until mid-February formed a long-distance escort of the invasion force attacking the Dutch East Indies. In the meantime, on January 21-28, she escorted a convoy to Davao on Mindanao, Philippines. On February 16, *Maya* and *Takao* left Palau and headed for the Moluccan Sea and Banda, to provide a distant cover for Japanese aircraft carriers which attacked Port Darwin, Australia on February 19. Since February 25, a force including *Takao*, *Atago*, *Maya* and two destroyers of the 4th Destroyer Division headed for the area near the Dutch harbour of Tijlatjap at the southern coast of Java. Their objective was to protect the invasion forces and eliminate the Allied ABDA naval forces. The invasion began on March 1, and on that day Vice Admiral Kondō's forces sank first enemy ships, Dutch motorship *Toradja* and British auxiliary minesweeper HMS *Scott Harley*. The next day, the cruiser *Maya* along with the destroyers sank an old British destroyer HMS *Stronghold*, spotted earlier by reconnaissance floatplanes. *Maya* expended as many as 653 203.2 mm shells to send her to the bottom. The surrender of Allied forces on Java on March 9, marked the end of the first phase of planned Japanese operations, therefore, on March 11, *Maya* and *Takao* departed Celebes and headed to their home port of Yokosuka. The ship was refitted by April 14. Small-calibre guns were added and their type and calibre were unified (25 mm). Following the refit, the cruiser *Maya* headed south of Yokosuka, to Owase Bay. On May 1, the cruiser along with *Takao* headed for Hiroshima Bay and remained at Hashirajima anchorage in Kure. The ships began training in preparation for a new operation. On May 20, *Takao* and *Maya* were attached to the Second Mobile Force under command of Rear Admiral Kakuji Kakuta, which was a part of Vice Admiral Boshirō Hosogaya's Fifth Fleet. The objective was to attack Dutch Harbor and to invade the Aleutians (AL Operation), in order to divert the American attention from the main objective, which was the capture of Midway (MI Operation). The cruisers left Kure on May 22, and headed towards the north of Honshu, to Ominato naval base, in the Mutsu Bay. They arrived there on May 25. They departed two days later with the tankers *Fujisan Maru* and *Nissan Maru*, three supply vessels, two destroyers, and headed for Paramushiro in the Kuril Islands, arriving on June 2. On the next day, the entire strike force put to sea. The carrier-based planes were to attack military installations at Dutch Harbor and Unalaska Island. During the operation both cruisers launched their reconnaissance floatplanes to locate U.S. warships reported by returning Japanese planes. The floatplanes failed to find them, but were intercepted by Curtiss P-40 Warhawks stationed on Umnak Island, which in turn were looking for Japanese warships. Two Japanese planes were shot down and two more, heavily damaged, performed emergency landings in the vicinity of their ships. Following the attack on Dutch Harbor, the ships remained in the area. On June 5, Japanese forces were attacked by U.S. bombers and managed to shoot down one of the planes. The force, joined by larger units detached from the forces operating near Midway, protected the landings on Attu and Kiska in the Aleutians. The ships remained in the area until June 20, however, since there was no American opposition, Japanese ships returned to their bases. The cruisers *Takao* and *Maya* arrived at Ominato on June 24. Four days later they departed to join a force including aircraft carriers, which secured a second convoy to Kiska. The force remained in the area near the Aleutians between July 4 and 7, then the ships returned to their bases. The cruisers *Maya* and *Takao* headed for Hajirashima anchorage and arrived there on July

Starboard side.

13. Following the defeat at Midway, where the Japanese lost 4 large aircraft carriers, the Japanese Admiralty made numerous plans to convert battleships and cruisers into aircraft carriers. One of such designs called for the conversion of the "Takao" class and other heavy cruisers into aircraft carriers within nine months. These conversions were to carry about 30 planes, but finally the idea was abandoned.

August 1942 to December 1942

Due to U.S. landings at Tulagi and Guadalcanal in the Solomon Islands, the 4th Cruiser Division, along with other units, left Kure on August 11 and headed for Truk. For the first time the ship received a new, three-seat Aichi E13A1 Jake floatplane. On August 20, the KA Operation was launched with the objective to recapture Tulagi and Guadalcanal. Vice Admiral Kondō's ships left Truk and reinforced Vice Admiral Nagumo's Third Fleet. For days later, an aerial battle took place, near the eastern coast of the Solomon Islands. A few days before the battle the Americans completed the construction of the airfield at Guadalcanal, which had been started by the Japanese. Therefore, the strategic situation in the area did not look good for the Japanese. The cruiser *Maya*, along with other units, returned to Truk on September 5. Five days later, warships of the Second and Third Fleet put to sea again and headed south, towards the Solomon Islands. U.S. forces were not engaged and on September 20, the ships were ordered to return to the Carolines, where they arrived on September 23. On October 11, the 4th Cruiser Division left Truk again to support Vice Admiral Nagumo's forces, which were supposed to defeat U.S. aircraft carriers and support the Guadalcanal offensive. The cruisers *Maya* and *Myōkō*, along with light escort units, were assigned to bombard Henderson Field, Guadalcanal, to reduce the risk of attacks by the planes stationed there. The action took place at night of October 15-16. The cruisers fired 450 Type 3 and 462 Type 91 main calibre rounds respectively. On October 26, there was a carrier battle, known as the battle of the Santa Cruz islands. The cruiser *Maya* did not participate and, following the battle, the ships of the opposing forces returned to their respective bases. Warships of both Japanese fleets returned to Truk on October 30. Due to intensive fighting in the Solomon Islands area and losses sustained by the Eight Fleet, on November 3, the cruisers *Maya* and *Suzuya*, assisted by destroyers, left Truk and headed for the Shortland Islands, near the eastern coast of Bouganville. They were to reinforce Vice Admiral Gun'ich Mikawa's forces. They arrived there on November 5. Eight days later, a force composed of heavy cruisers: *Chōkai*, *Maya*, put out to sea with the objective to bombard and put Henderson Field out of action in order to facilitate the safe passage of a large convoy of 11 troop ships heading for Guadalcanal. On the way, the cruisers launched their reconnaissance floatplanes to drop flares and light targets for the artillery. The bombardments were performed by three cruisers: *Maya*, *Chōkai* and *Suzyua*. On November 14, at about 09.30, the cruiser *Maya* was attacked by two dive bombers of the VB-10 from the aircraft carrier USS *Enterprise*. The bombs missed the ship, but the wing of one of the Dauntless planes, probably hit by anti-aircraft fire, struck the mainmast and crashed into the mid-ship. Burning fuel ignited about twenty 120 mm shells stored near the gun mount. Torpedoes were jettisoned as a precautionary measure. The situation was put under control and the ship reached Shortland on her own. Thirty-seven people were killed and two 120 mm gun mounts, a searchlight platform and a 25 mm anti-aircraft gun mount were destroyed. On the next day, *Maya* left Shortland and steamed to Truck. Following provisional repairs, she arrived at Yokosuka on January 5, 1943.

January 1943 to July 1943

The ship had been repaired and sent to Paramushiro. On March 7, *Maya* and *Nachi* departed to escort convoy I-21 heading for Attu Island. They returned six days later. They put to sea again on March 23, to provide cover for another convoy heading for Attu. On the way to the Aleutians, on the morning of March 27, 1943, near the Komandorski Islands, the cruiser *Maya* played an important role in the battle with TG16.6 under command of Rear Admiral Charles H. McMorris. The cruiser fired a total of 904 main calibre shells (*Nachi* fired 707 and USS *Salt Lake City* 832), scoring several hits on the U.S. heavy cruiser, sustaining light damage herself. After the battle, the ship returned to Yokosuka on April 3. On April 15, following the overhaul, the cruiser began her monotonous service in the northern waters of the Empire. On April 27, *Maya* headed for Shimushu Island. Due to the American invasion of Attu, which had begun on May 11, the cruiser put to sea, but on May 15 she returned to the Kuriles and then steamed to Ominato, where she remained between June 21 and July 1. *Maya* and *Nachi* were supposed to take part in the evacuation of the troops stationed at Kiska. They put to sea on July 10, but the action was cancelled due to bad weather conditions and the ships returned to Paramushiro.

August 1943 to March 1944

Analysing the battles fought around the Solomon Islands, the high command of the Japanese Navy with the Navy Technical Department decided to strengthen the anti-aircraft defence of the ships, ordering the first wartime modernization. As part of it, air-search radar was installed, and in

order to increase the anti-aircraft firepower, additional twin 25 mm gun mounts were installed, bringing the total number of barrels to 16 (8xII). Steel windshield was installed in the front section of the bridge tower to protect its glazed, upper levels. *Maya* remained at the shipyard from August 6 until September 15. Then, loaded with troops, she steamed for the Caroline Islands, reaching Truk naval base on September 20. Following the air raid of the American carrier-based planes against Wake Island and the Marshall Islands on October 5 and 6, a strong task force of Japanese warships left Truk and headed for Eniwetok Atoll. Admiral Mineichi Koga, anticipating a second strike, for three days, (October 23 to 26) patrolled the area south of the Wake Island, ready for a counter strike, but to no avail. On November 3, the 4th Division, with the cruisers *Suzuya*, *Mogami* and *Chikuma*, left Truk and headed from Rabaul to reinforce Japanese forces in that area. That decision had fatal consequences for the Japanese Navy. On November 5, Americans launched a daring attack against the base at Rabaul. Ninety-seven planes from the aircraft carriers USS *Saratoga* and USS *Princeton* inflicted heavy damage on Japanese warships. Six heavy, two light cruisers and 3 destroyers were damaged. The cruiser *Maya* was hit by a single 500-pound bomb dropped from a Douglas SBD-5 Dauntless dive bomber. It hit the aircraft deck and exploded above No.3 engine room, starting a raging fire, which was not extinguished until the next day. The explosion and the subsequent fire killed a total of 70 crew members and 60 more were wounded. The ship remained immobilized and after the fire had been extinguished, emergency repairs were commenced and lasted until November 11. *Maya* left New Britain and headed for Truk, reaching the base there three days later. Further repairs were made by the repair ship *Akashi* and on November 28, the ship headed back to Japan and arrived there on December 5. It was decided that within the Second Wartime Modification both *Maya* and *Chōkai* would be rebuilt into anti-aircraft cruisers. The modification of the *Maya* took part at Yokosuka Navy Yard and lasted from December 5, 1943, until April 4, 1944. The No.3 main battery turret was removed, anti-aircraft armament was replaced by mounting new guns and their total was increased from four 120 mm mounts to twelve 127 mm ones. Light anti-aircraft battery was increased from sixteen 25 mm guns to 48 with the addition of thirty-six moveable 13 mm machine gun mounts. The number of torpedo tubes was increased from eight to sixteen and a depth charge rack was fitted aft. Stability, buoyancy and anti-torpedo protection were increased. Bridge structure, hangar and aft superstructure were considerably rebuilt. New radar equipment was installed. The ship received a Type 22 surface-search radar and the mattress spring antenna of Type 21 radar was replaced. A hydrophone was also installed in the bottom of the hull.

Since April 1944 until the sinking

On April 16, following the completion of her modification, *Maya* left Yokosuka and steamed to Kure. Then, along with the battleship *Yamato* and the destroyers screen, they headed for Manila in the Philippines, finally arriving there on April 28. On June 11, 1944, the Americans began air raids against the Mariana Islands, with the main objective being the capture of the most important islands of the archipelago: Saipan, Tinian and Guam. On the very next day, Adm. Soemu Toyoda, expecting an invasion, issued an order to start preparations for Operation A-GO, which turned out to be a devastating defeat of the Japanese navy. During the operation, the cruiser *Maya* along with the battleship *Haruna*, screened the aircraft carrier *Chiyoda*. In the late afternoon hours, on June 20, the task force was attacked by a group of Grumman TBF-1 Avenger bombers. The cruiser was slightly damaged by near-misses and her hull was flooded with approximately 120 tons of water. *Maya* steamed to Yokosuka and arrived there on June 25. The repairs were commenced immediately. She underwent her Third Wartime Modification, which included the increase of the anti-aircraft armament. Eighteen single 25 mm gun mounts were installed, which increased the total number to 66 pieces. There is no information concerning the fate of machine guns. However, the authors believe that due to their inefficiency in battle, they were removed and replaced with new 25 mm mounts. New No.13 radar was installed with its characteristic dipole array antenna on the foremast. The ship left Yokosuka on July 14 and moved to Kure and then to Singapore. The Japanese navy had a plan for a decisive naval battle in defence of the Philippines called SHO ICHI (Victory 1), therefore the operation is better-known as the SHO-1-GO. Battle of Leyte Gulf was a series of four naval engagements which took place in the waters of the Philippine Islands between October 23 and 26. These were, the battle of the Sibuyan Sea, the battle of Cape Engaño, the battle of Surigao Strait and the battle of Samar. Japanese forces were divided into groups, each one was assigned a different objective. The most important First Mobile Strike Force (also known as the "Center Force"), under command of Vice Adm. Takeo Kurita, was divided into three sections. The most important for this narrative is the first section which comprised the 1st Battleship Division (*Yamato*, *Musashi*, *Nagato*), 4th Cruiser Division (*Atago*, *Takao*, *Chōkai*, *Maya*) and 5th Cruiser Division (*Myōkō*, *Haguro*). Kurita's ships departed from the base at Brunei at about 21.00, and according to plan, headed north to enter the waters around Palawan Island through the passage of the same name. These waters had been patrolled since October 1, by the U.S. submarines USS *Darter* (SS-227) and USS *Dace* (SS-247). They spotted Japanese ships shortly after midnight, on October 23. Both submarines, undetected by Japanese destroyers, took positions to attack both columns of the Japanese force. At dawn, at about 05.32 of the local time, USS *Darter* fired six torpedoes at *Atago* from a distance of only 980 yards. Then, after taking a turn, the submarine fired another four torpedoes from her stern tubes from the distance of 1550 yards at the second ship in the column, the cruiser *Takao*. *Atago* was hit by four torpedoes at 05.33 and sank 19 minutes later, taking with her 360 officers and sailors. Vice Adm. Kurita, saved himself by jumping into the water. *Takao*, despite taking evasive manoeuvres, was hit a minute later by two torpedoes, which heavily damaged the ship and put it out of action. Commander of the USS *Dace*, LtCdr Bladen Claggett, took advantage of the confusion, and at 05.55, from a distance of 1800 yards, fired six torpedoes at the third ship in the Japanese column. It was the cruiser *Maya*, although, Claggett was convinced that the massive silhouette was that of a "Kongo" class battleship. Two minutes later, four Mark 14, 530 mm torpedoes, each with a warhead filled with 292 kg of Torpex (explosive material about 50% more powerful than TNT), hit the port side of the cruiser. The first exploded in the forward chain locker, the second below the base of No.1 turret, the third in No.7 boiler room and the final fourth in No.3 engine room. The extensive flooding caused the ship to list 30° to port. The fire reached forward magazines and caused a tremendous explosion. The cruiser went down at 09°27' N, 117°23' E, at 06.05, taking with her 336 crew members, including her commander, Captain Ranji Ōe. Destroyer *Akishimo* managed to rescue a total of 769 men, including 47 officers and transferred them to the battleship *Musashi*. It was not the end of *Maya*'s tragedy. Kurita's force was attacked by planes launched from U.S. aircraft carriers on October 24, even before Ozawa's aircraft carriers were discovered. Numerous air attacks against the Japanese strike force, later known as the battle of the Sibuyan Sea, ended in sinking of the battleship *Musashi*. Before the battleship went down, the destroyer *Shimakaze* took on board 635 survivors from the cruiser *Maya*. Therefore, the cruiser lost a total of 470 men (according to some sources 479 men) out of 1105 complement. The cruisers *Maya*, *Atago* and *Chōkai* were stricken from the Navy List on December 20, 1944.

Operational commanders of the heavy cruiser Maya

The following list includes all commanders of the Japanese heavy cruiser *Maya*. Their ranks while they performed the duty on board the cruiser, as well as the final ranks they were promoted to, are given. The names are written in Japanese style, with surname first. Dates are in British English format (DD.MM.YYYY).

30.06.1932 - 1.12.1932, Captain Morimoto Jō (Rear Admiral, 23.07.1886 - 1.11.1969);

1.12.1932 – 15.11.1933, Captain Yamamoto Kōki (Vice Admiral, 20.04.1887 - 24.01.1958);

15.11.1933 - 15.11.1934, Captain Nīmi Masaichi (Vice Admiral, 4.02.1887 - 2.04.1993);

15.11.1934 - 28.10.1935, Captain Ozawa Jisaburō (Vice Admiral, refused the promotion to Admiral, Commander-in-Chief of the Imperial Japanese Navy, 2.10.1886 - 9.11.1966);

28.10.1935 - 1.12.1936, Captain Moizumi Shin'ichi (Vice Admiral, 5.04.1888 - 26.11.1969);

1.12.1936 - 15.11.1937, Captain Ōshima Kenshirō (posthumously promoted to Vice Admiral, 20.03.1889 - 9.03.1938);

15.11.1937 - 15.11.1938, Captain Suzuki Yoshi (Vice Admiral, 15.11.1890 – killed 21.11.1944);

15.11.1938 - 15.11.1939, Captain Nakahara Yoshimasa (Vice Admiral, 3.04.1892 - 23.02.1944);

15.11.1939 - 15.04.1941, Captain Ōsugi Morikazu (Vice Admiral, 11.03.1892 – executed 28.08.1948);

15.04.1941 - 11.08.1941, Captain Izaki Shunji (posthumously promoted to Vice Admiral, 5.02.1892 – killed 12.07.1943);

11.08.1941 - 30.09.1942, Captain Nabeshima Shunsaku (Rear Admiral, 10.09.1892 - 28.04.1948);

30.09.1942 - 16.10.1943, Captain Matsumoto Takeshi (Rear Admiral, 14.04.1896 - 14.5.1962);

16.10.1943 - 26.12.1943, Captain Katō Yoshirō (posthumously promoted to Rear Admiral, 28.03.1894 – killed 25.02.1945);

26.12.1943 - 23.10.1944, Captain Ōe Ranji (posthumously promoted to Rear Admiral, 18.08.1897 – killed 23.10.1944).

Evaluation of the anti-aircraft cruiser conversion

The "Takao" class cruisers, similarly to the majority of the Imperial Japanese Navy units, were built as offensive, therefore, the Admiralty did not attach much significance to their defensive equipment. New anti-torpedo bulges added during the reconstruction improved the safety of the ship, however, they did not prevent her demise. Such bulges were added to the *Takao* and *Atago* long before the outbreak of the war, and *Maya* was scheduled to be so modified in 1941. When the war broke out, the anti-aircraft armament of all the cruisers of that class had been considered too weak. All the attempts to remedy the situation made by the Admiralty and Navy Technical Department, were introduced too late and were inadequate in the face of the growing threat. Transformation into an anti-aircraft cruiser was achieved mainly by the reduction of the main battery (from 10 to 8 guns, through removal of the No.3 gun turret) and the increase of the anti-aircraft armament. The decision to replace four 120 mm guns with twelve 127 mm mounts was a correct one in every respect. In theory, it allowed for a barrage of anti-aircraft fire to be laid at a safe distance from the ship. However, it must be noted, that her sister ships, rebuilt before the war, had already been armed with 8 such guns in four twin mounts. It

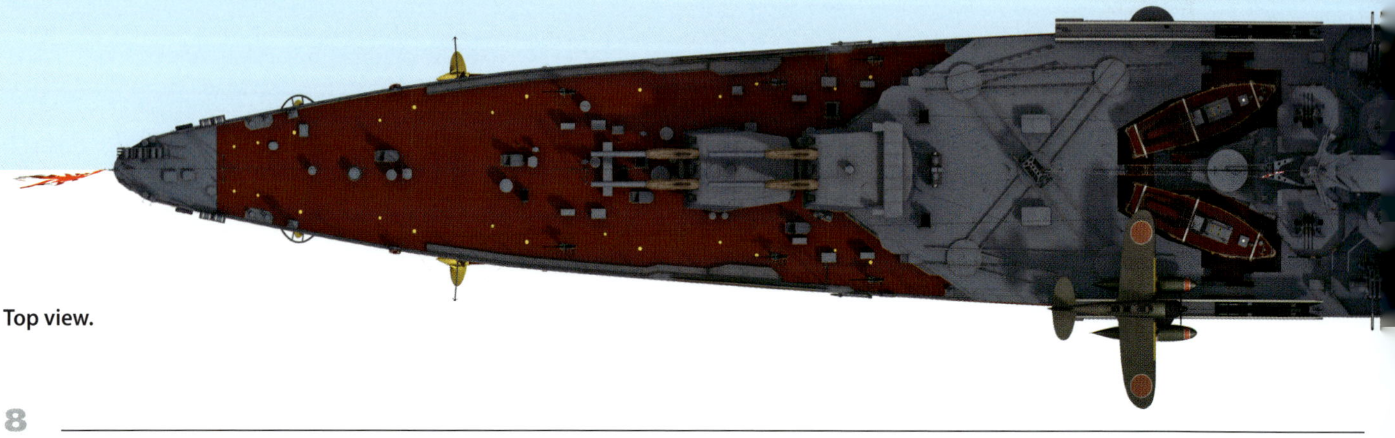

Top view.

is puzzling, why, despite availability problems, the 10 cm L/65 Type 98 anti-aircraft guns, designed for the large "Akizuki" class destroyers, were not used. Unfortunately, the quantity was not equal to quality. The Americans had been using VT proximity fuses on a large scale for over a year, while in Japan the idea was not even discussed. The use of radar for fire control was also an issue. It was introduced in the Japanese navy at the turn of 1944/1945, when the majority of its warships had already been sunk, however, only general-purpose radars were used. The efficiency of the American guns of the same calibre was approximately ten times higher than that of the Japanese ones (according to American data, the use of the VT fuses alone increased the probability of shooting down a plane three-fold). The 25 mm guns, the primary small-bore anti-aircraft armament of the Japanese navy, had already been ineffective. They may have been considered adequate at the beginning of the war, although they had not been mounted in sufficient numbers, but it 1944 they became useless. Feeding ammunition via a fixed magazine was slow, time-consuming and labour-intensive, which translated into a low continuous rate of fire and constant involvement of the gun crew in the reloading process. Fire control was automated and efficient up to a maximum target speed of approximately 380 km/h. When a plane was moving faster the operator had to be involved. Moreover, the recoil was excessive and a single mount itself was too high for an average operator (at that time Japanese males were approximately 1.6 m tall). All those deficiencies in the face of absolute American domination in the air and the introduction of new, faster and armoured planes, doomed the 25 mm gun as an anti-aircraft weapon. Mounting of machine guns as anti-aircraft armament seems to escape logical explanation. For comparison's sake, it may be interesting to present the armament of American "Baltimore" class heavy cruisers, which were being built at the time of *Maya*'s transformation. They were armed with nine 203.2 mm guns (3 x III), twelve 127 mm guns (6 x II), forty-eight 40 mm guns (12 x IV) and twenty 20 mm guns (20 x I). It is apparent that their light anti-aircraft battery, which consisted of 40 mm Bofors guns, was more powerful and thus, its barrage fire was effective at a greater distance from the ship. The increase of small-bore anti-aircraft armament under no circumstances improved the offensive capability of the ship. It did, however, increase the number of men needed to operate it, which finally amounted to higher losses, but the Japanese imperialism could not care less. The Japanese should have tried to find other types of weapons or invest into innovative radar equipment. However, cooperation between Japan and Germany, the only country able to help them in that respect, did not go smoothly. Therefore, after 1944, the Land of the Rising Sun was destined to lose.

Authors' note

We have created this publication together and we both share responsibility for its contents. We are aware of the fact that some of our ideas will not appeal to everyone. However, we have tried to be logical and spent hours discussing aspects which had been disregarded by others. We have tried, with what little was available to us in the form of research material, to create a publication which would bring this beautiful ship to life in her final configuration as an anti-aircraft cruiser. The readers will probably be able to notice that in many cases, which we are painfully aware of, we had second thoughts concerning the appearance of the cruiser in July 1944. Available plans and drawings could hardly be considered as absolutely reliable, since they often contradict each other. Discrepancies also exist as far as dimensions, displacement, weight of certain components and dates marking the introduction of certain equipment are concerned. Who is right and who is wrong, is not for us to decide. Therefore, we do hope that the readers will show their understanding. We would also like to encourage those who possess information which could broaden our knowledge of the ship or help us eliminate errors in forthcoming publications to contact us at waldemar.goralski@wp.pl

General characteristics of the anti-aircraft cruiser *Maya* (June 1944)

Standard displacement	13.139 t (13.350 t)
Normal displacement	15.159 t
Length overall	203.76 m
Length between perpendiculars	192.02 m
Beam (upper deck)	20.42 m
Beam	20.74 m
Hull height	10.93 m
Draft at normal displacement	6.44 m
Complement	1105 men
Main battery	8 x 203.2 mm (4 x II)
Heavy anti-aircraft battery	12 x 127 mm (6 x II)
Light anti-aircraft battery	66 x 25 mm (13 x III; 27 x I)
Machine guns	36 x 13.2 mm (36 x I)
	2 x 7.7 mm (2 x I)
Torpedo tubes	16 x 610 mm (4 x IV)
Depth charges	20
Aircraft facilities	2 catapults, 2 floatplanes
Power output	130.000 shp
Endurance	8.500 nm at 14 kn
	5.000 nm at 18 kn
Maximum speed	approx. 34.25 kn

Bibliography

"Japanese Cruisers of the Pacific War" - Eric Lacroix i Linton Wells II
"Krążowniki typu Myōkō" - Okręty Wojenne 20- Janusz Bukała
"The Imperial Japanese Navy Pictorial Book" No 6 Cruisers II- Kojinsha Japan
"History of United States Naval Operations in World War II"- Samuel Eliot Morison
"Silent Victory: The U.S. Submarine War against Japan"- Clay Blair, Jr.
Gakken Nr 16
combinedfleet.com
pwencycl.kgbudge.com

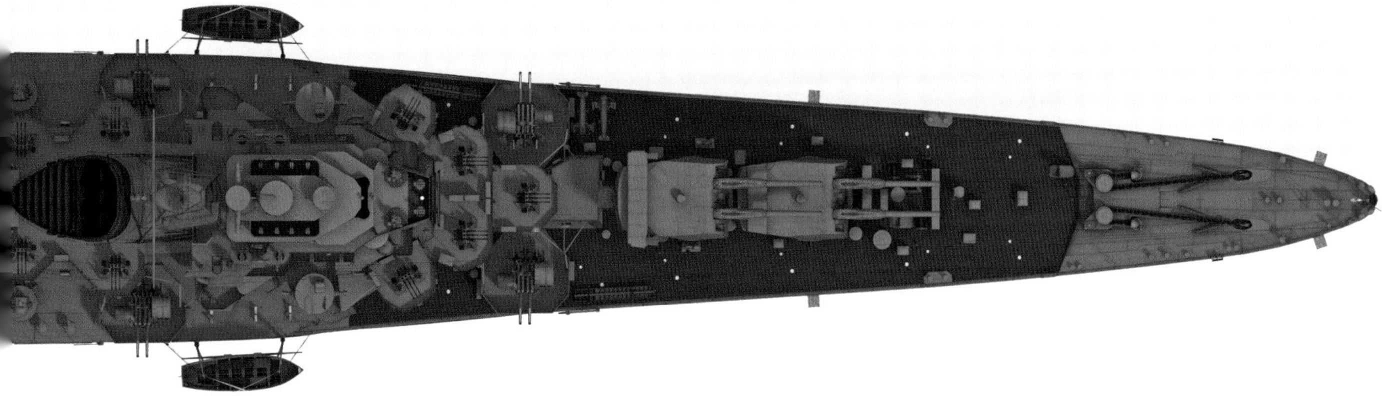

Bow view.

Stern view.

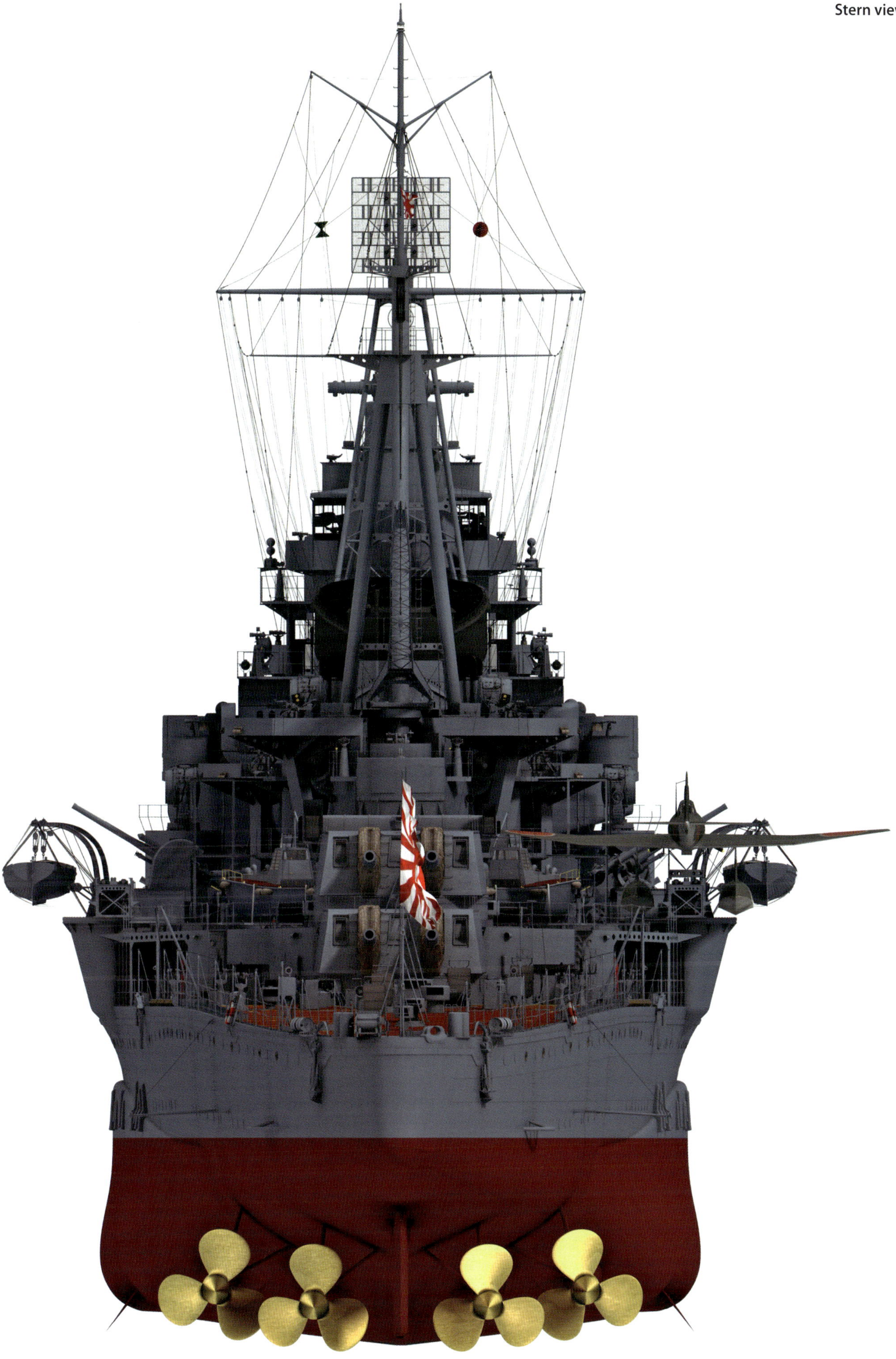

The cruiser *Maya* as seen from the bow. The Imperial chrysanthemum crest is clearly visible.

The bow section. Leadsman's and sounding platforms are seen on the sides.

Main battery turrets No.1 and No.2 with the command bridge, as seen from the forecastle.

Capstans and anchor chains.

Deck fittings in front of the main battery turret No. 1.

Forward main battery turrets. In the background the massive bridge tower can be seen.

Main battery 203 mm gun turrets.

Barbettes of the forward main battery turrets.

Bridge tower as seen from the deck.

Starboard side 127 mm anti-aircraft gun mount located at the base of the bridge tower.

Loading sequence of the 127 mm anti-aircraft gun.

Loading of a 127 mm anti-aircraft gun.

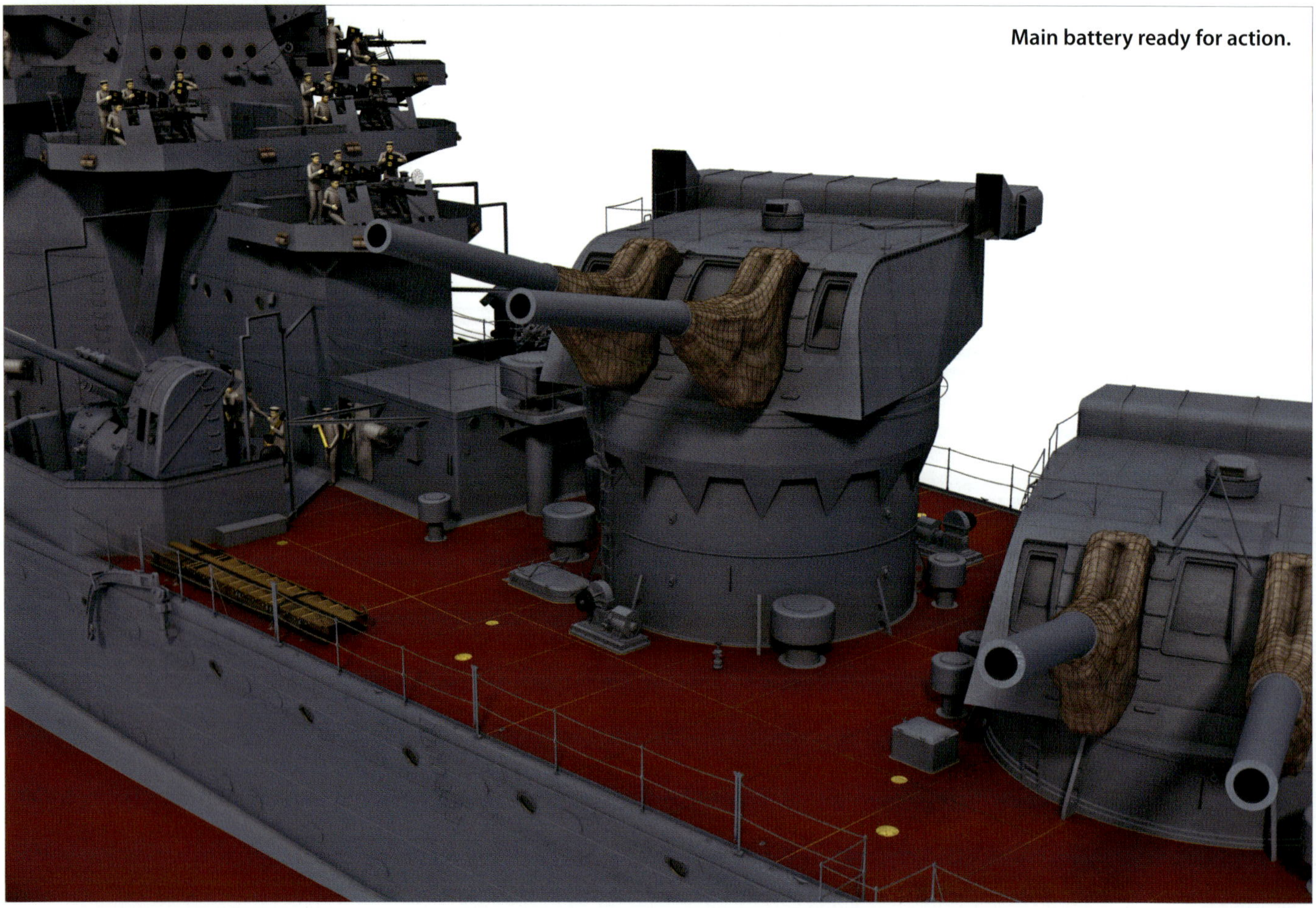

Main battery ready for action.

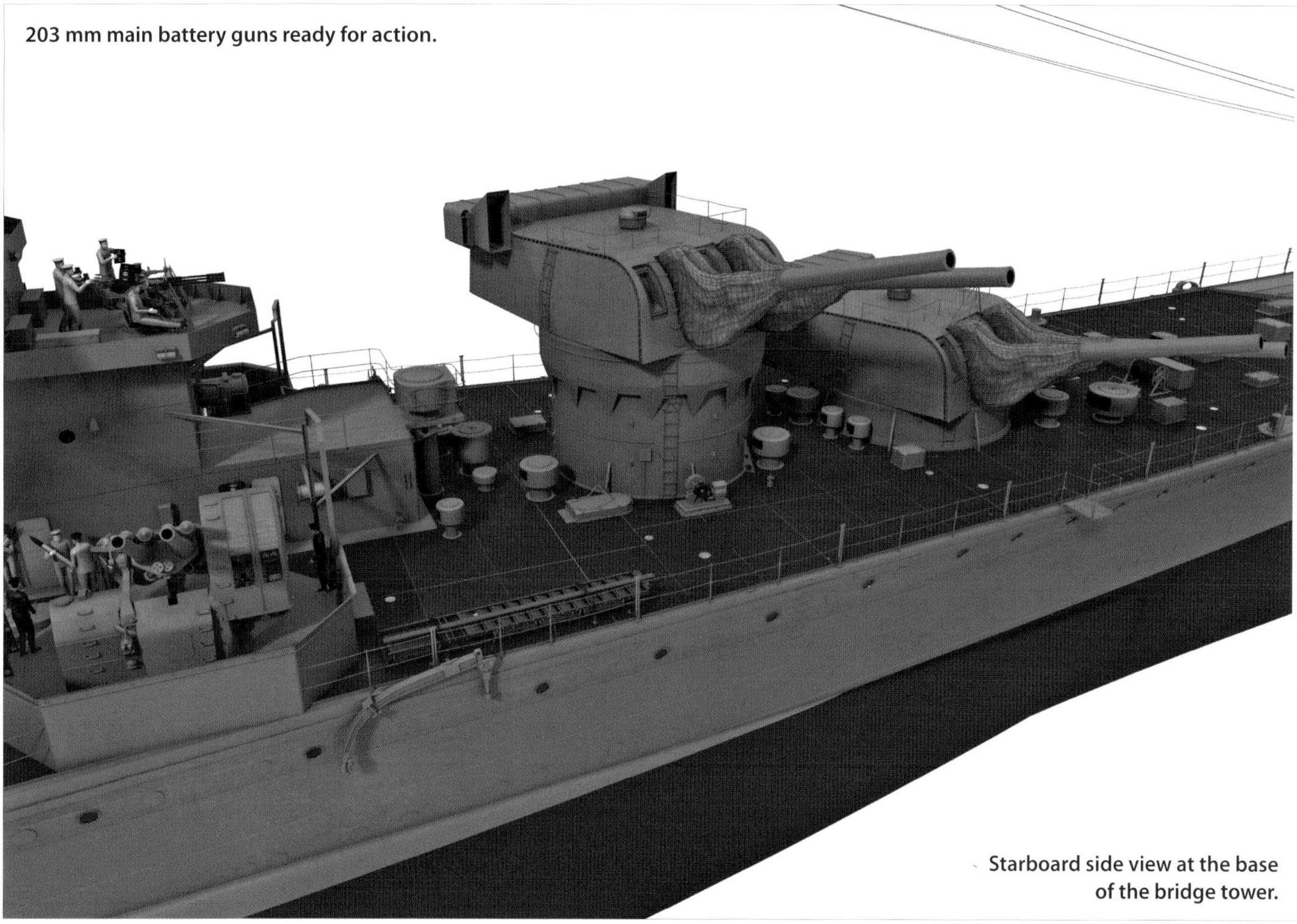

203 mm main battery guns ready for action.

Starboard side view at the base of the bridge tower.

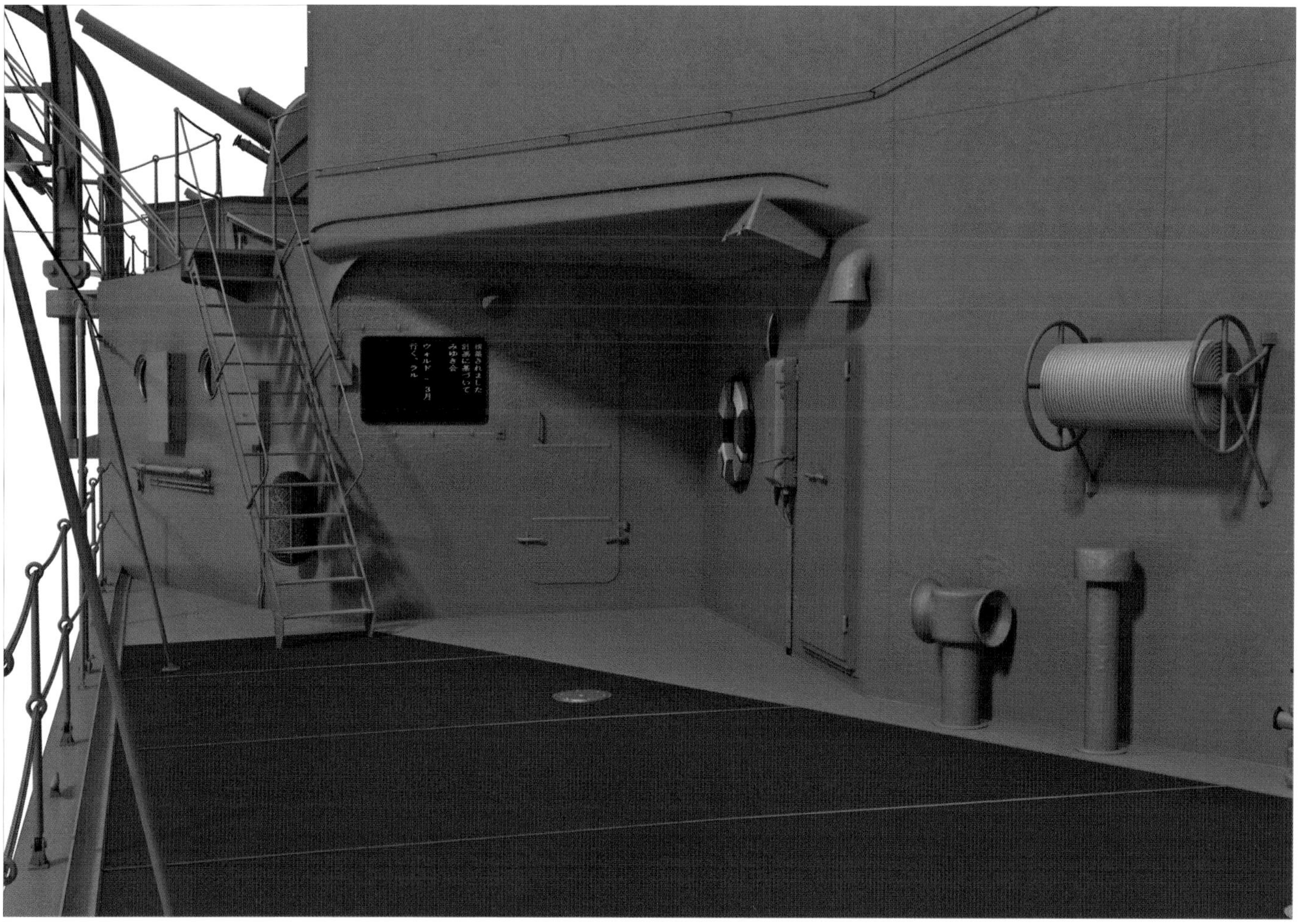

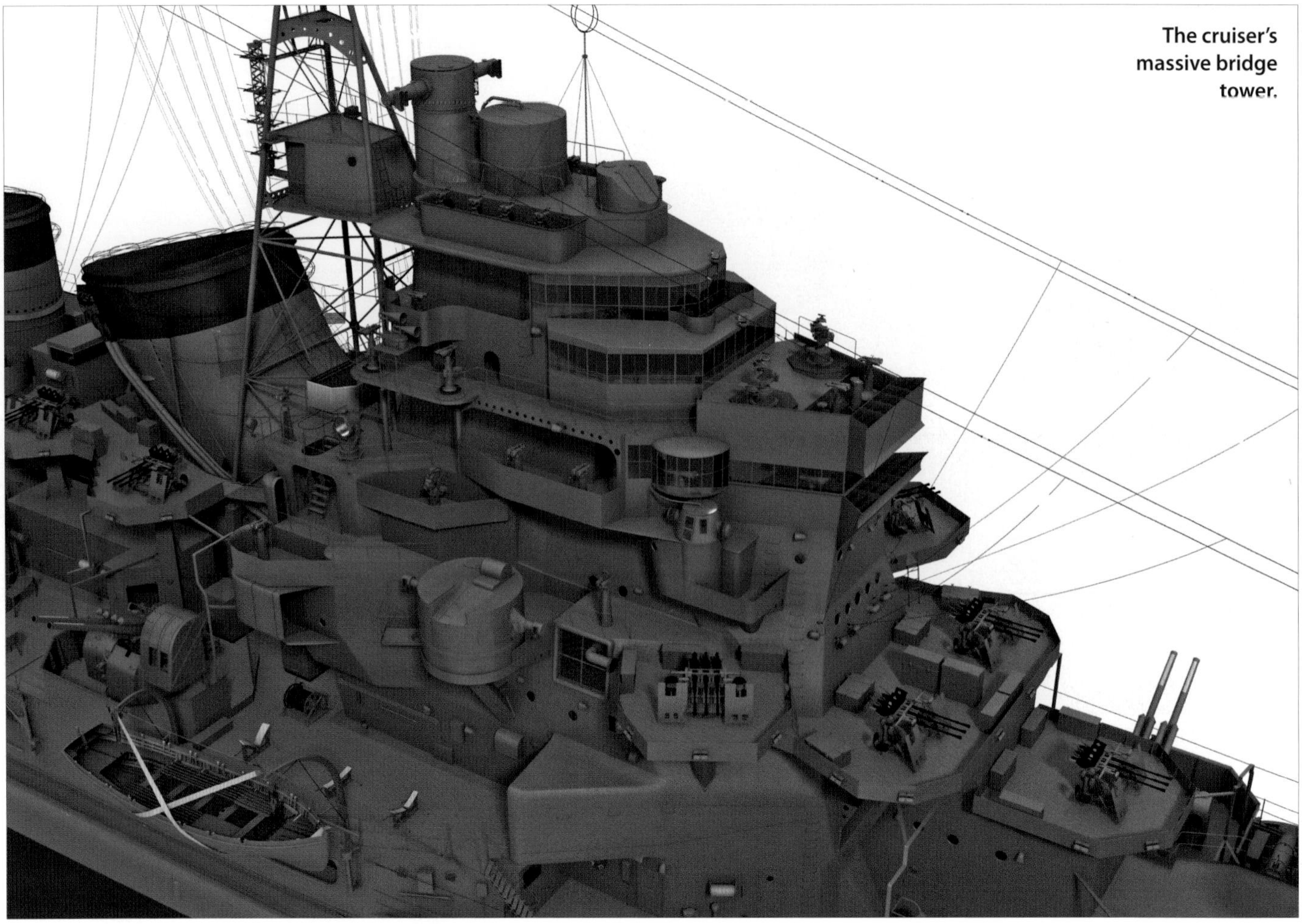

The cruiser's massive bridge tower.

Observation posts on the roof of the bridge tower.

Anti-aircraft command platform of the bridge tower.

The cruiser's forecastle, as seen from the anti-aircraft platform located on the front wall of the bridge tower.

A 127 mm anti-aircraft guns as seen from above.

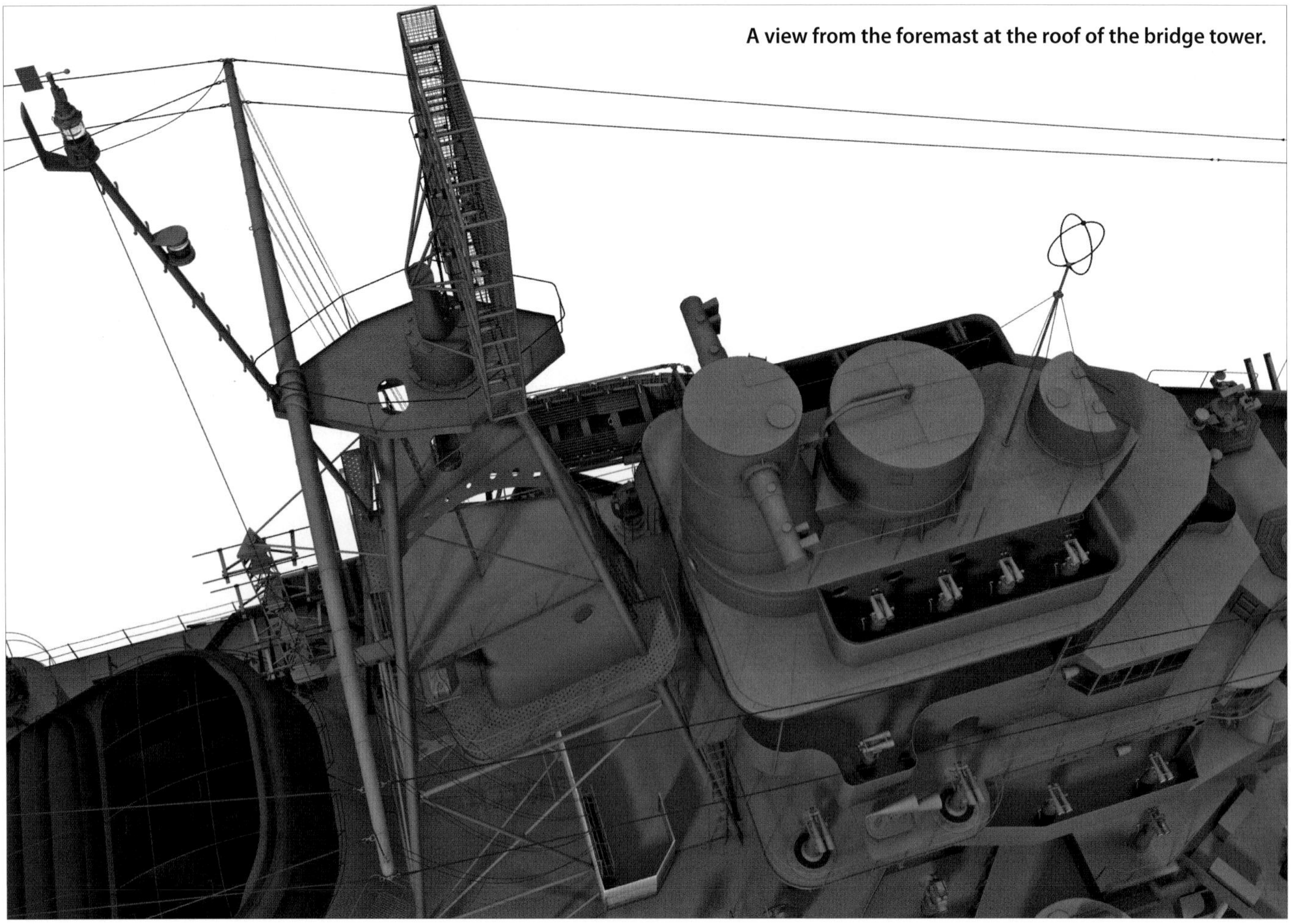

A view from the foremast at the roof of the bridge tower.

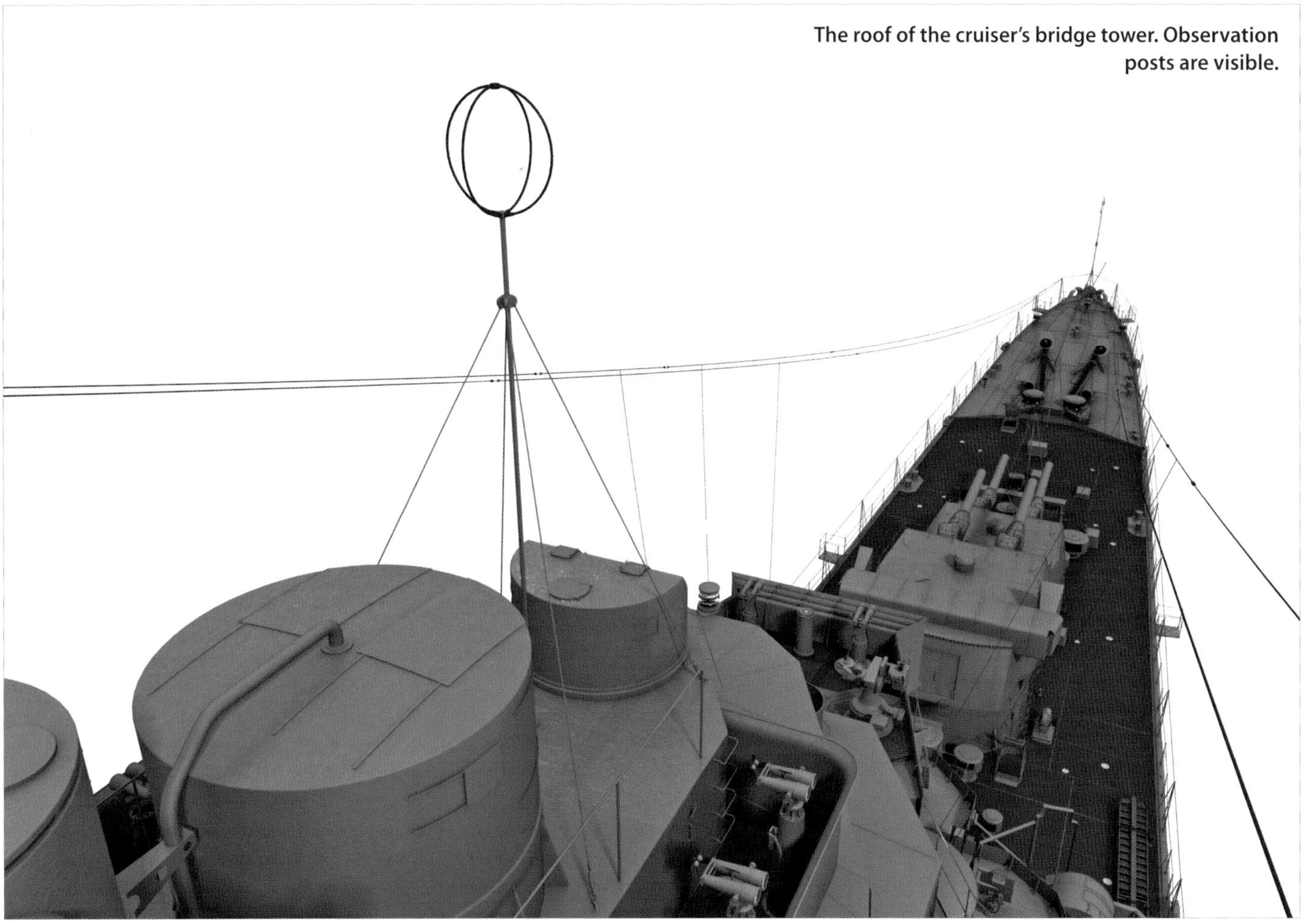

The roof of the cruiser's bridge tower. Observation posts are visible.

6-metre rangefinder atop of the bridge tower.

Type 21 radar atop the foremast.

Radar control room in the foremast.

Observation posts on the side of the bridge tower.

Type 94 4.5-metre rangefinder.

Observation posts atop the bridge tower.

A passage between the side and the bridge tower.

Midship as seen from the starboards side of the bridge tower. Triple 25 mm anti-aircraft gun mounts and the searchlight are visible.

Starboard side view at the base of the bridge tower.

9 m cutter on radial davits.

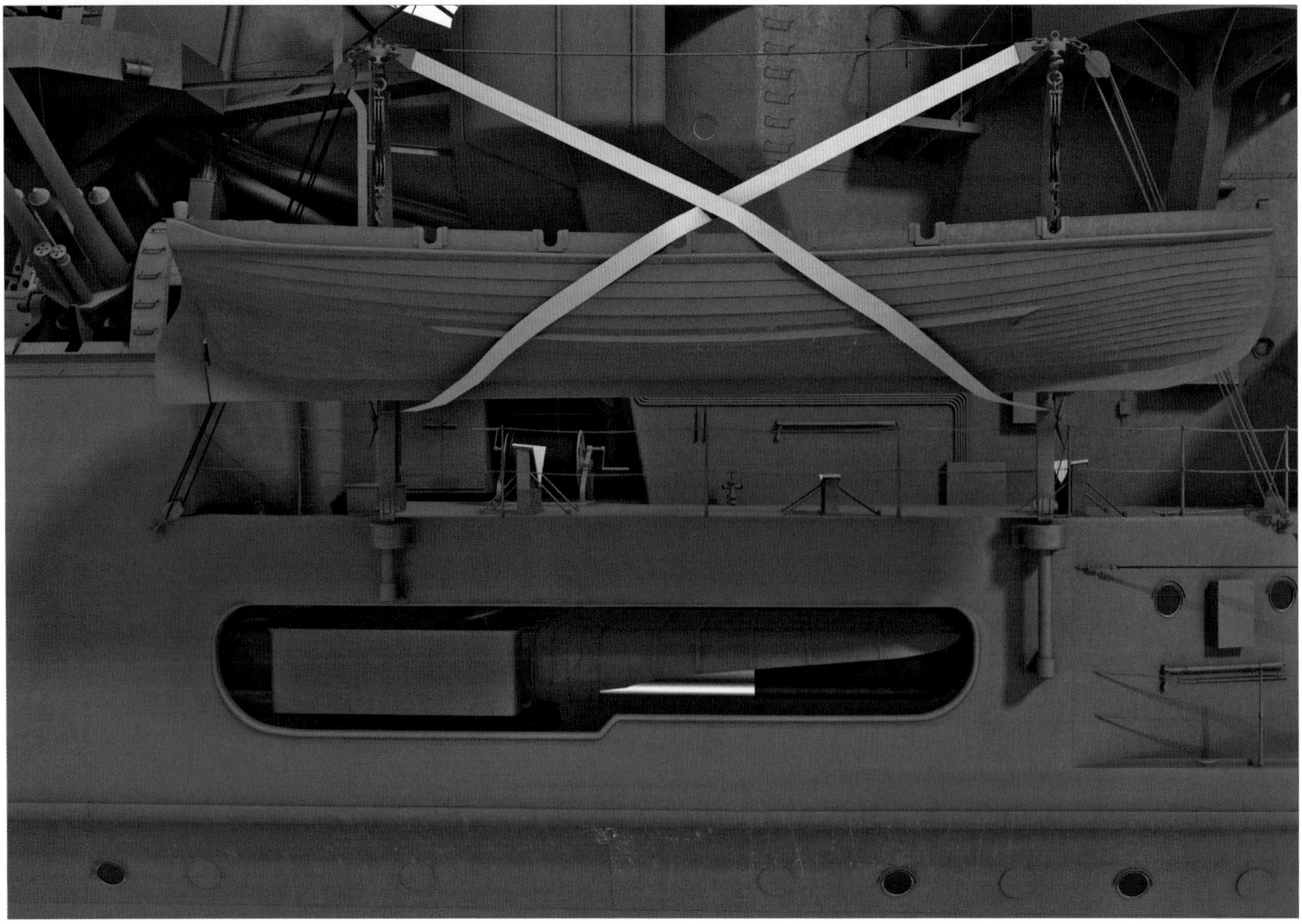

Midship 127 mm anti-aircraft gun mount.

Forward funnel and its fittings.

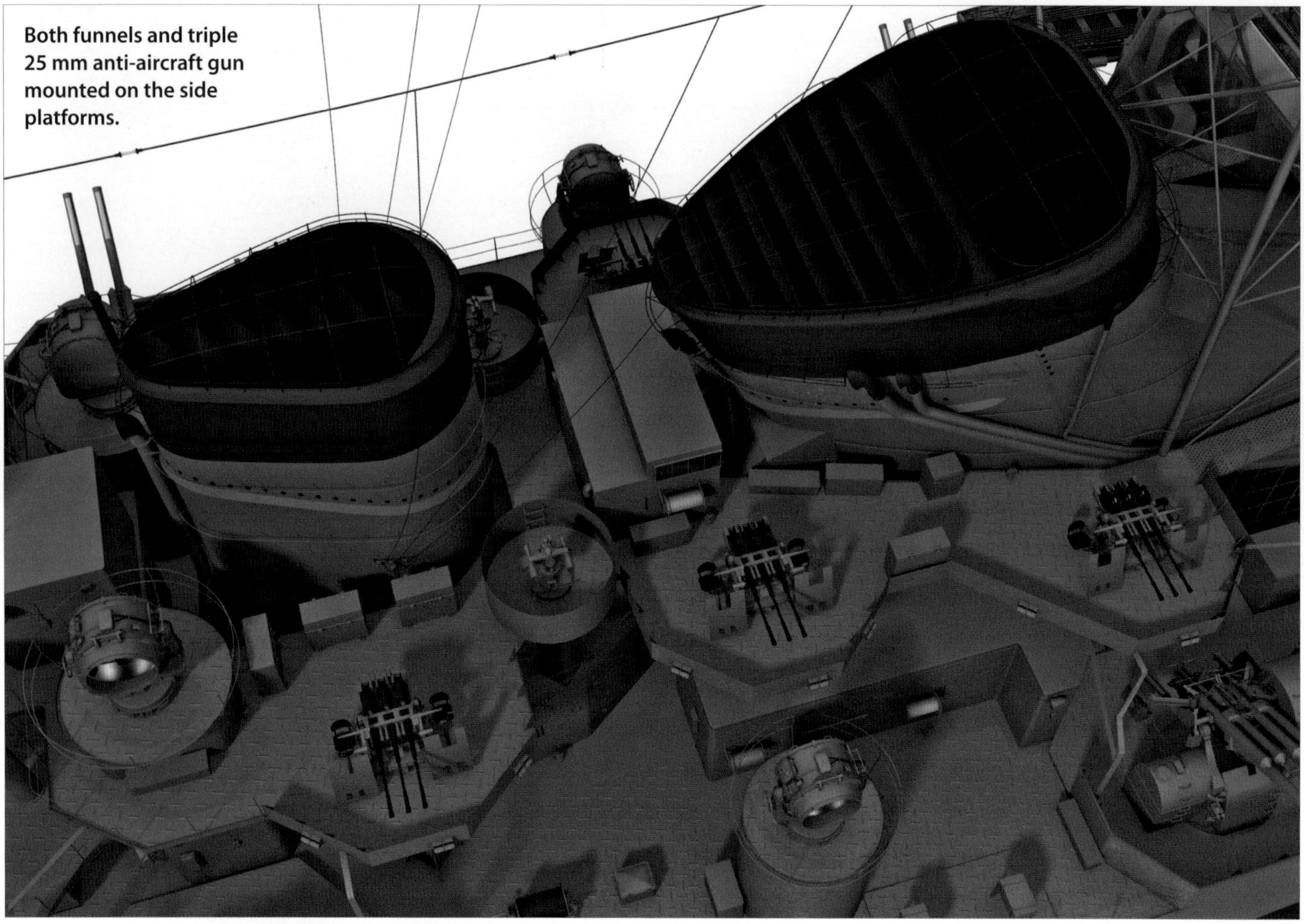

Both funnels and triple 25 mm anti-aircraft gun mounted on the side platforms.

Stern view of the bridge tower.

Anti-aircraft gun platforms on the starboard side of the forward funnel.

Air intakes on the sides of the bridge tower.

Starboard side triple 25 mm anti-aircraft gun mount.

Starboard side amidship. Spare torpedoes are visible.

Base of the searchlight amidship.

Provisional repairs station amidship.

Base of the forward funnel.

Mainmast as seen from the midship.

Foremast seen from astern.

Top of the mainmast.

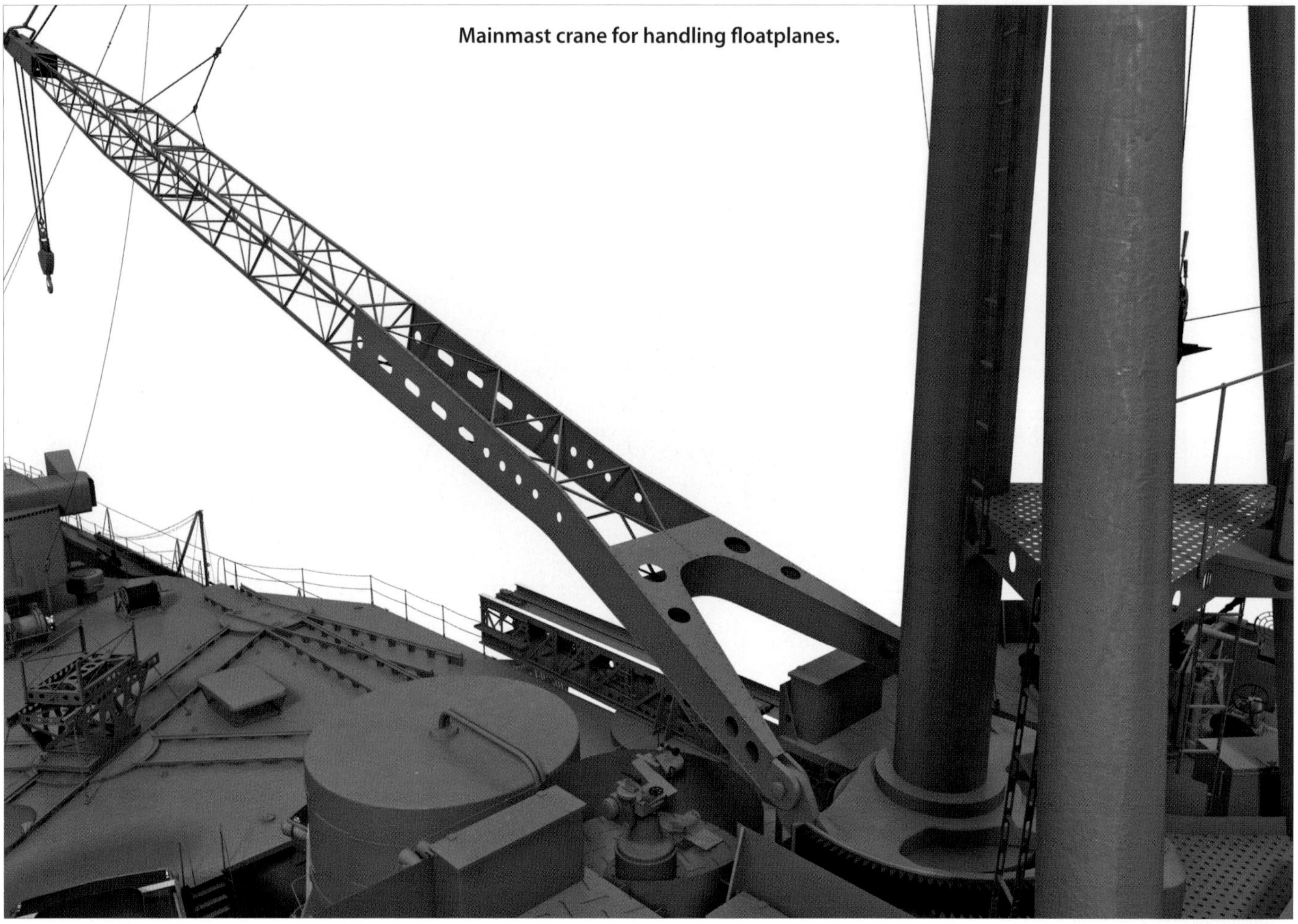
Mainmast crane for handling floatplanes.

110 cm searchlight on a platform at the side of the aft funnel.

Observation posts abaft the mainmast.

Midship section seen from astern. A starboard side 127 mm anti-aircraft gun mount can be seen in foreground.

11 m officers' barge stored atop an 11.5 m transport barge.

Inner part of the boat deck.

Aircraft deck as seen from the aft superstructure.

Ship motor boats as seen from the aircraft deck.

Aichi E13A1 Jake floatplane on the starboard catapult of the cruiser.

Starboard side midship view.

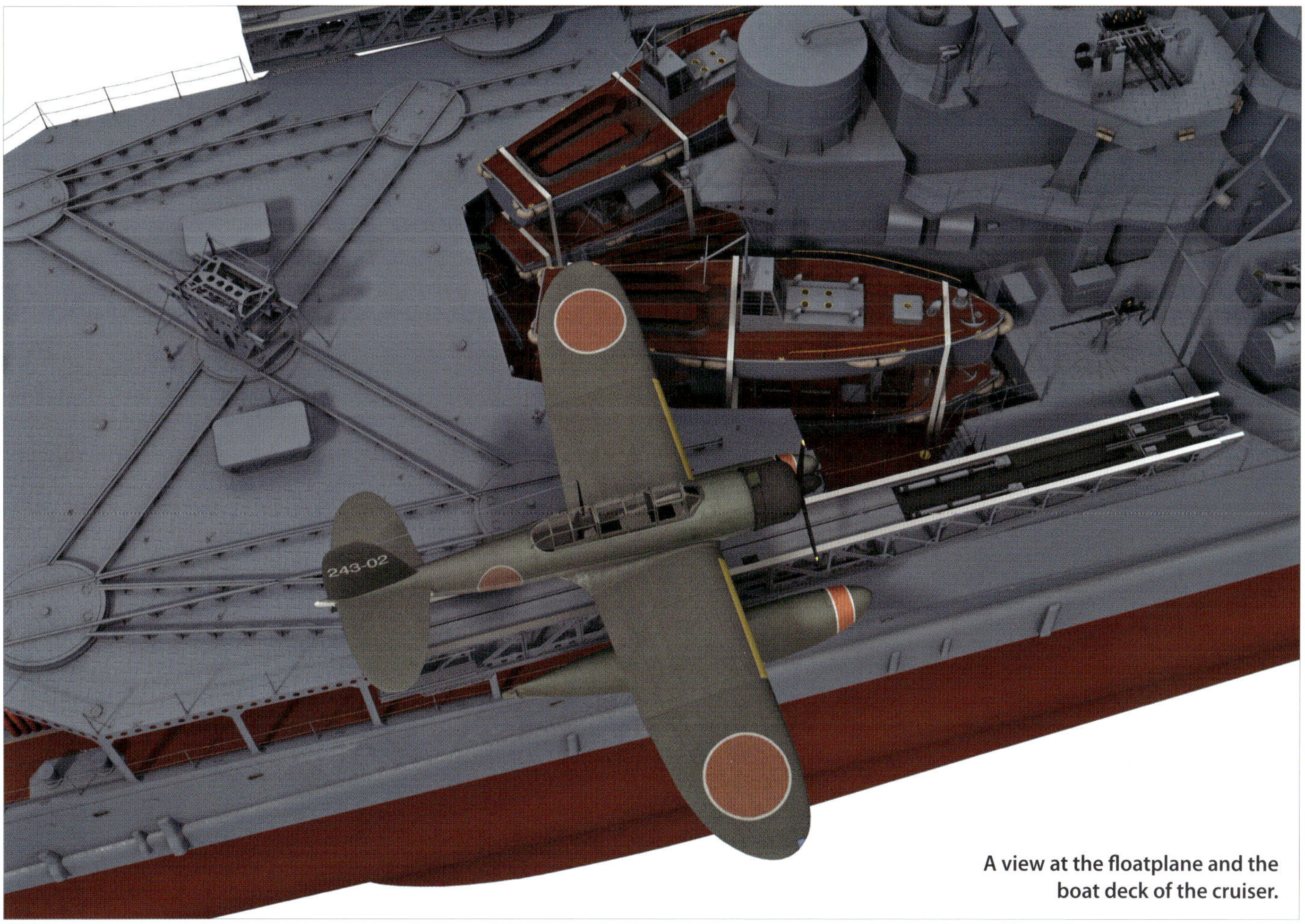

A view at the floatplane and the boat deck of the cruiser.

Quarterdeck as seen from the boat deck.

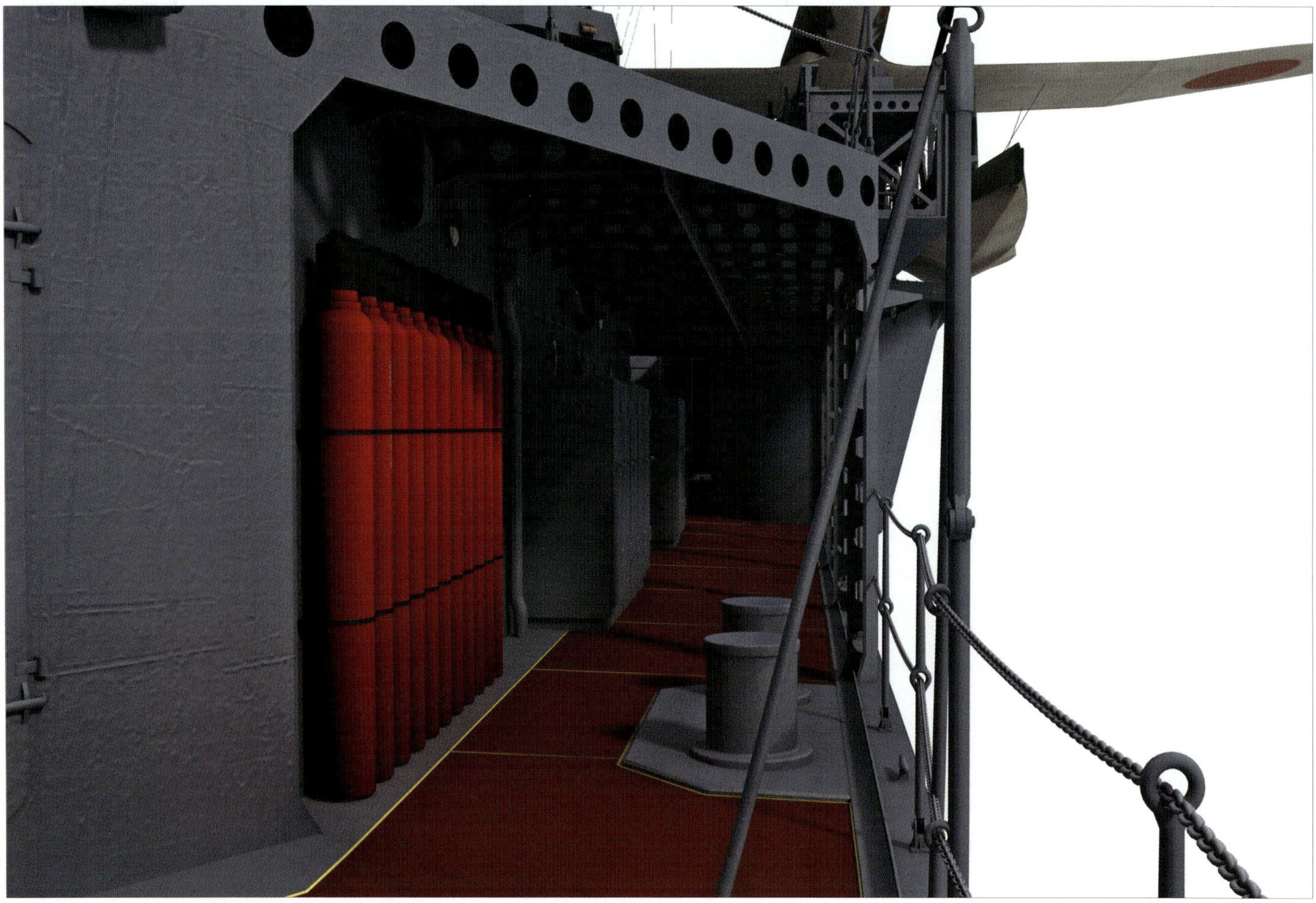

Compressed air tanks stored on the side of the superstructure, under the aircraft deck.

Quarterdeck as seen from the boat deck.

Aircraft deck.

Stern main battery turrets.

Aircraft deck as seen from astern.

A view from the quarterdeck at the starboard side of the cruiser.

Stern main battery turrets.

Main battery turrets seen from the quarterdeck.

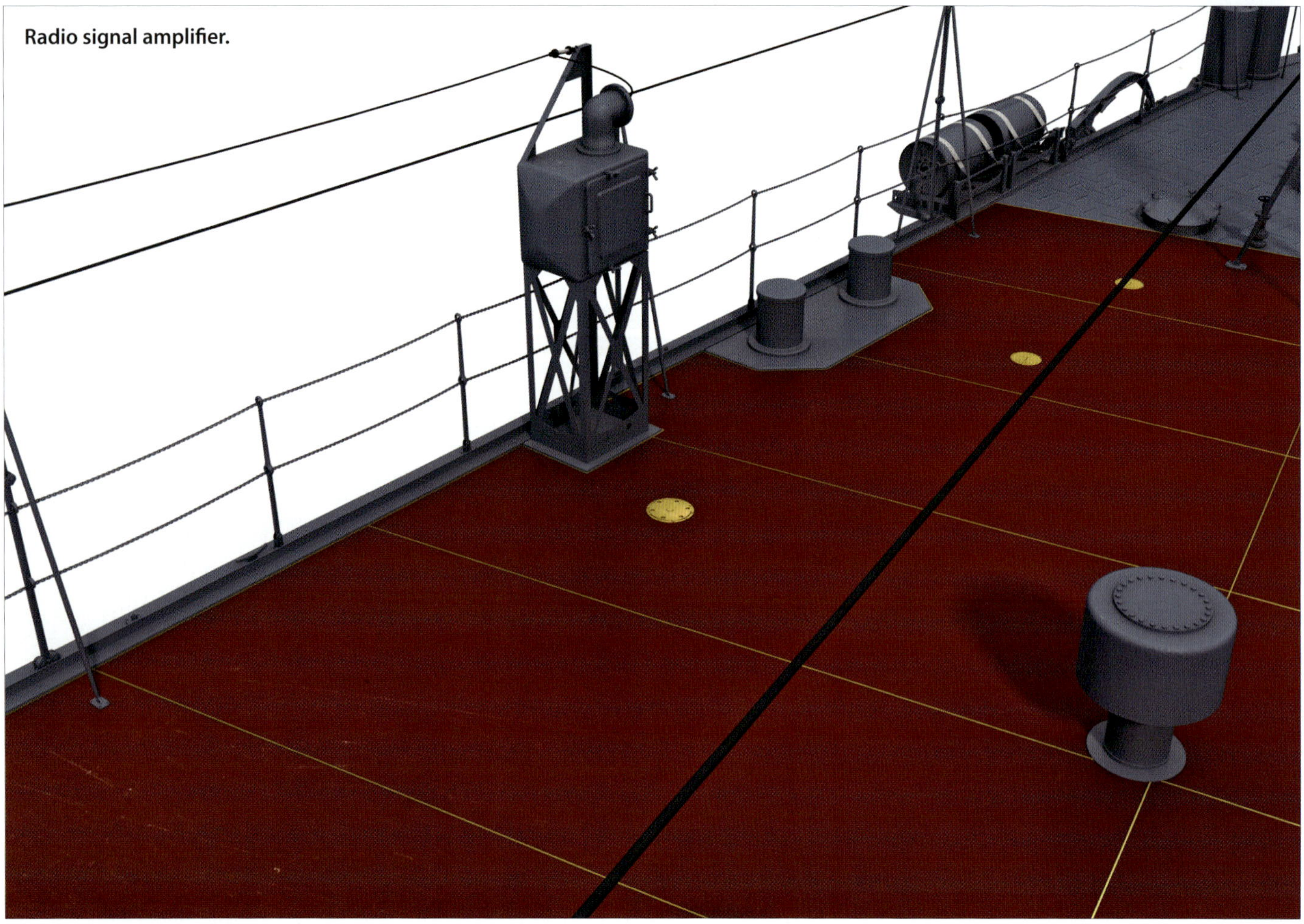

Radio signal amplifier.

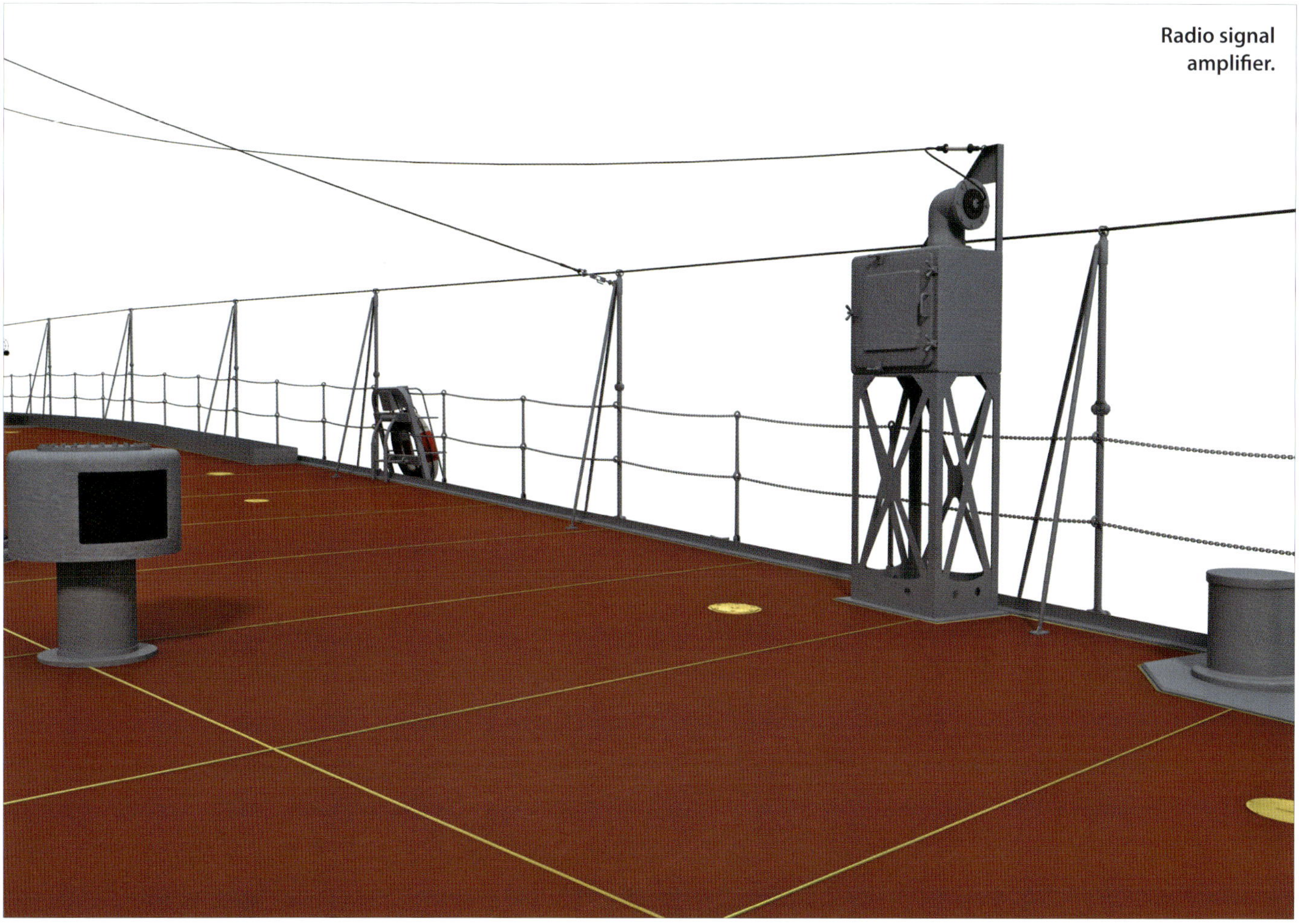

Radio signal amplifier.

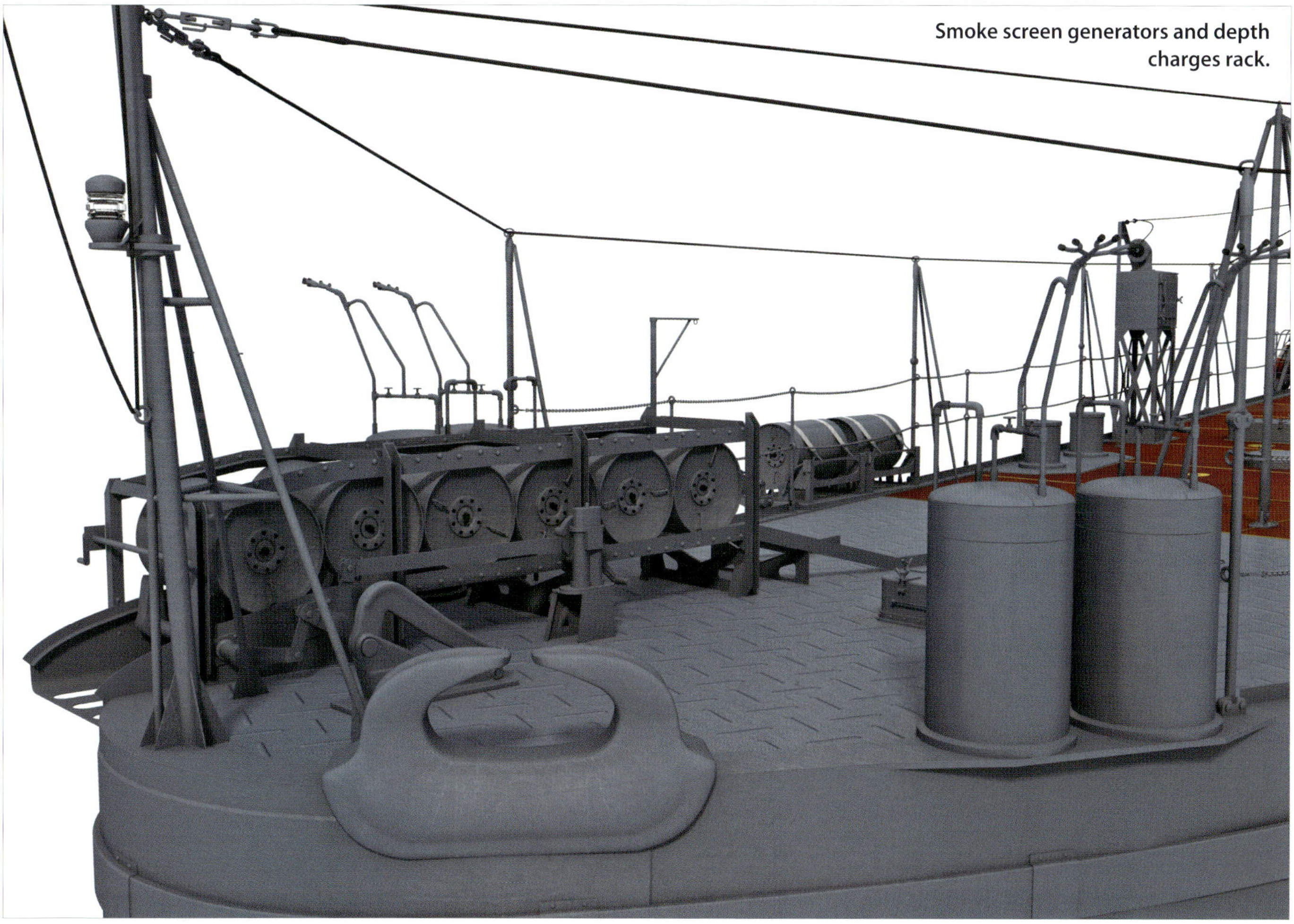

Smoke screen generators and depth charges rack.

Bow section. Ensign of the Empire of Japan is flown from the jackstaff.

Forward main battery turrets of the cruiser.

Superimposed main battery turrets.

Main battery turrets ready for action.

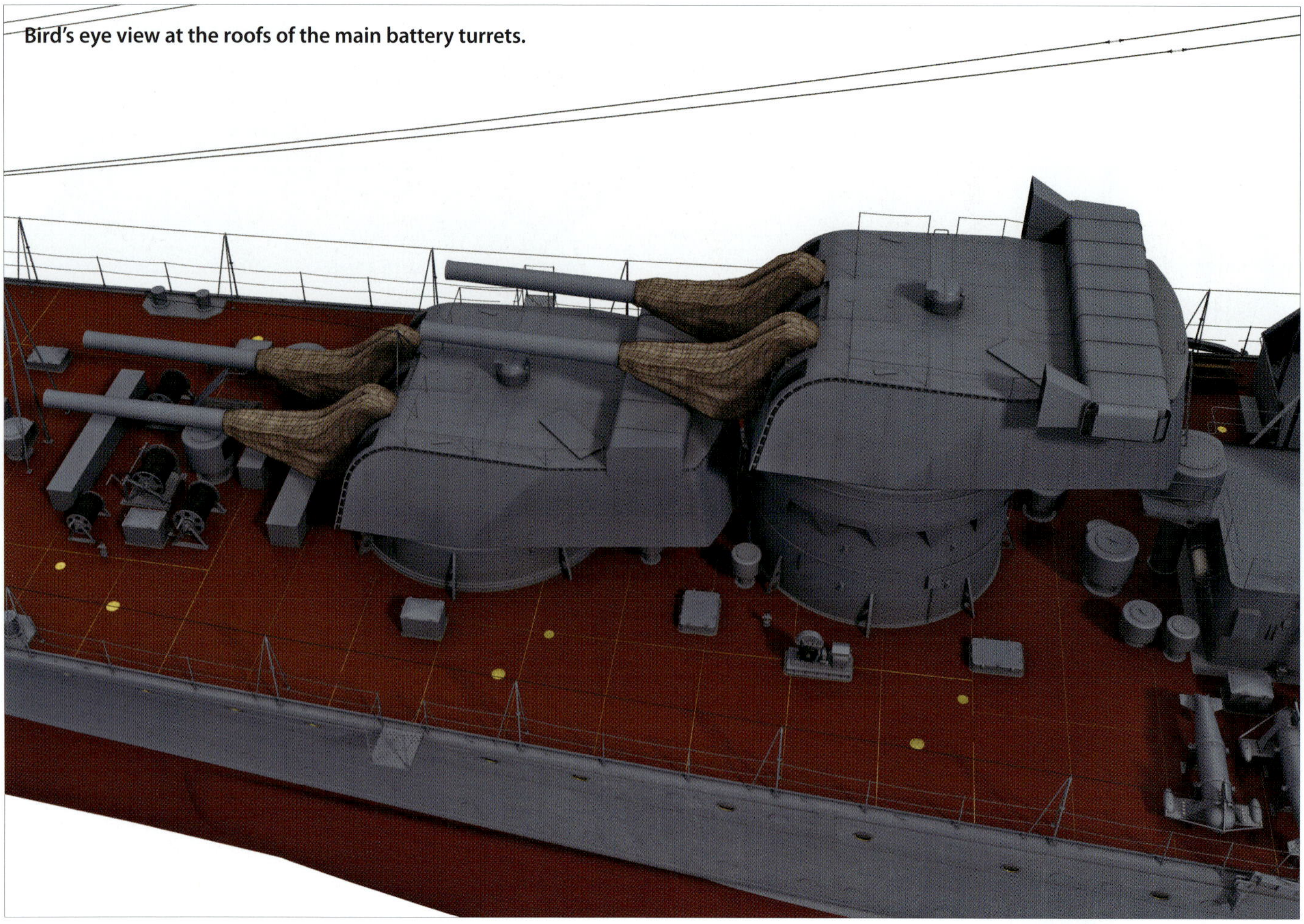

Bird's eye view at the roofs of the main battery turrets.

Port side of the bridge tower.

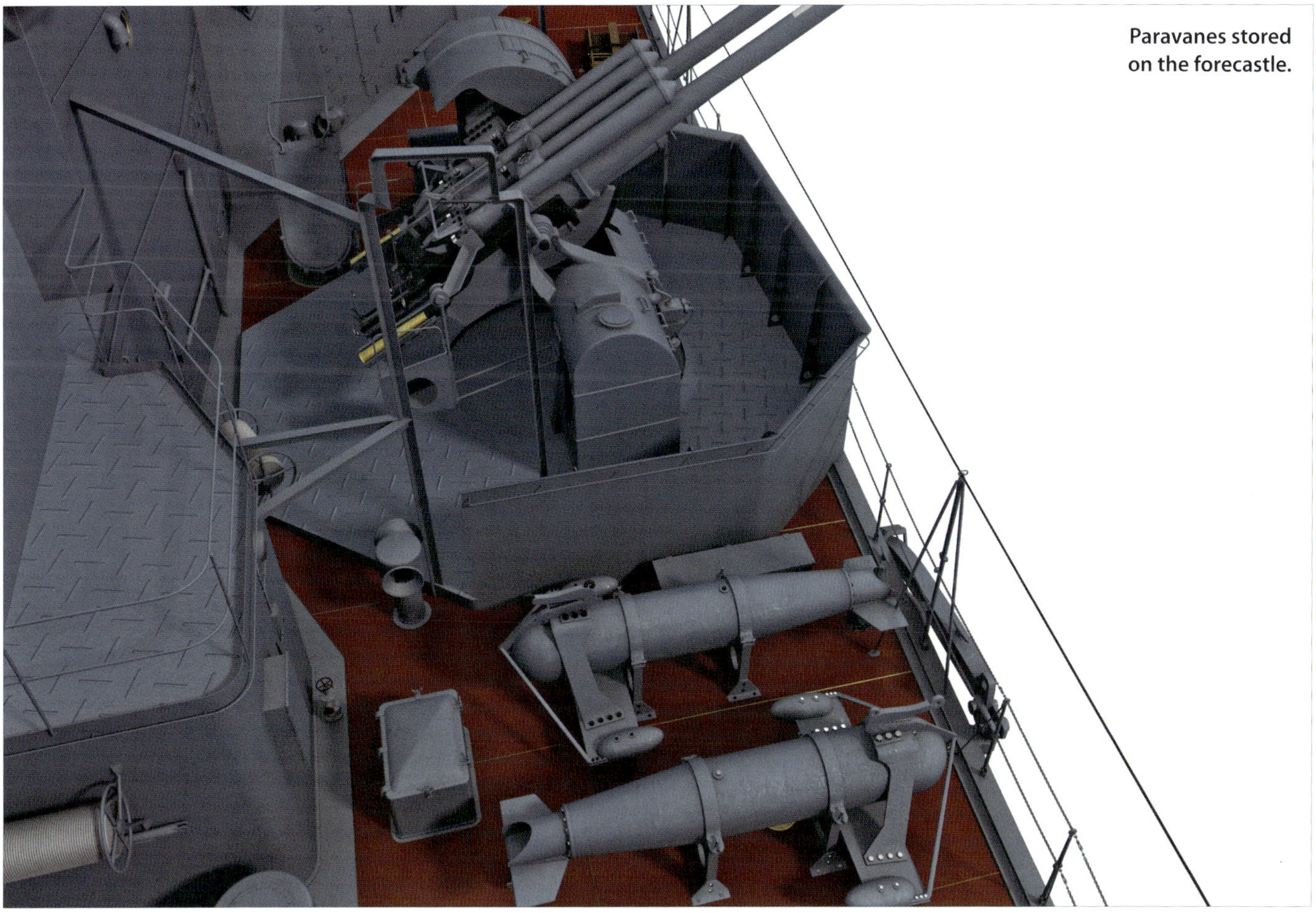

Paravanes stored on the forecastle.

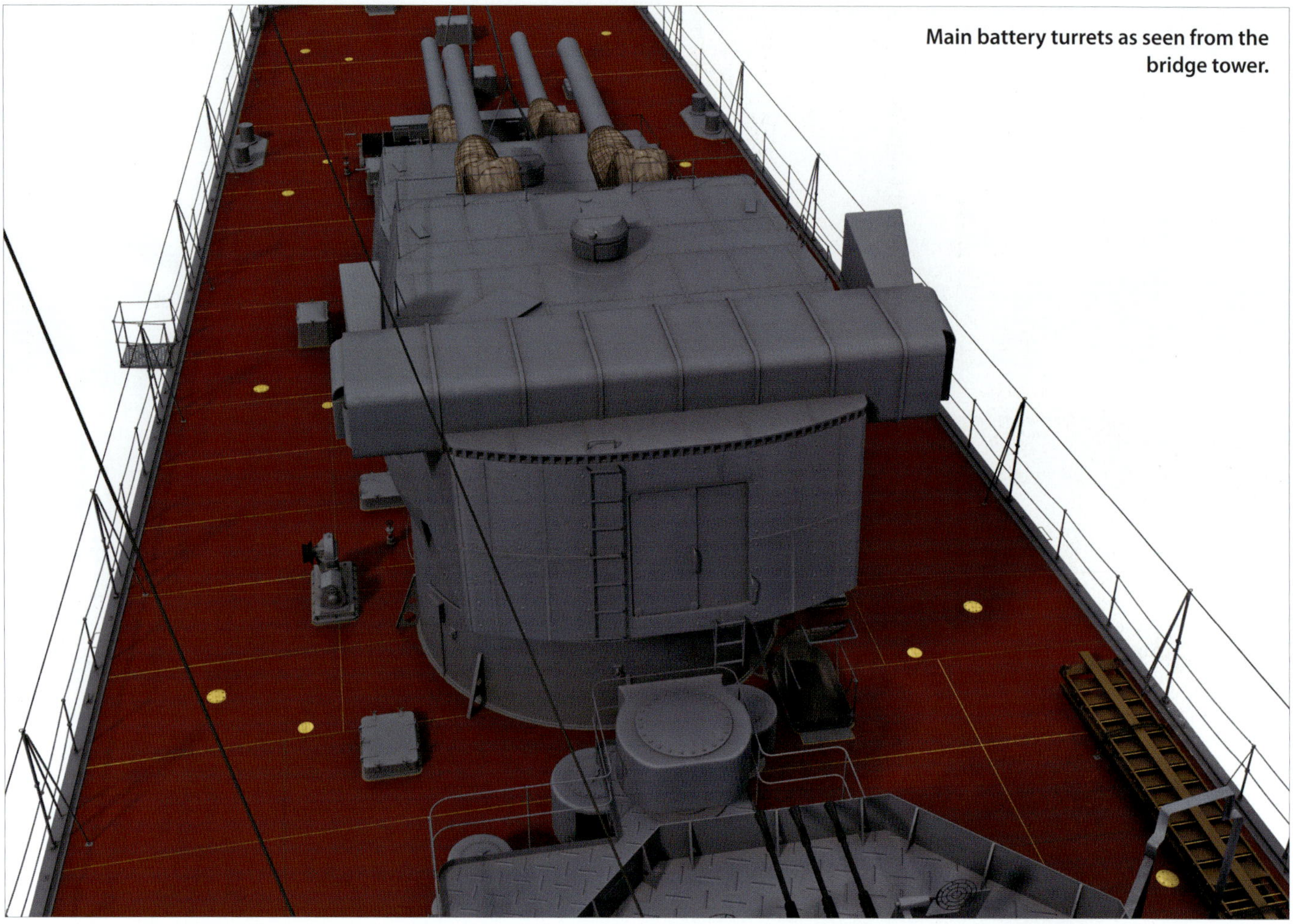

Main battery turrets as seen from the bridge tower.

The massive bridge tower.

Anti-aircraft gun platforms on the front wall and sides of the bridge tower.

Bridge tower seen from port astern.

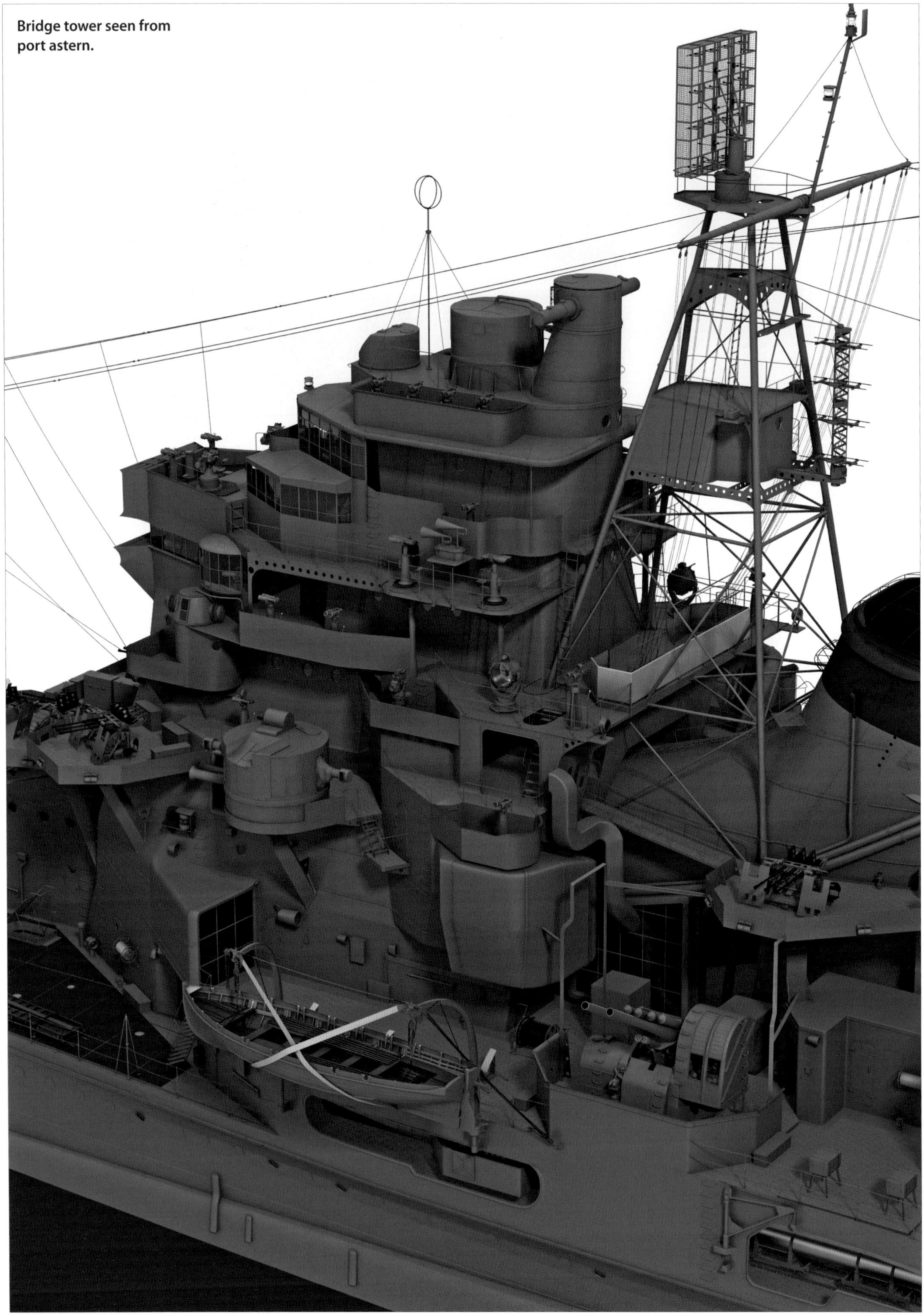

A port bow view of the bridge tower.

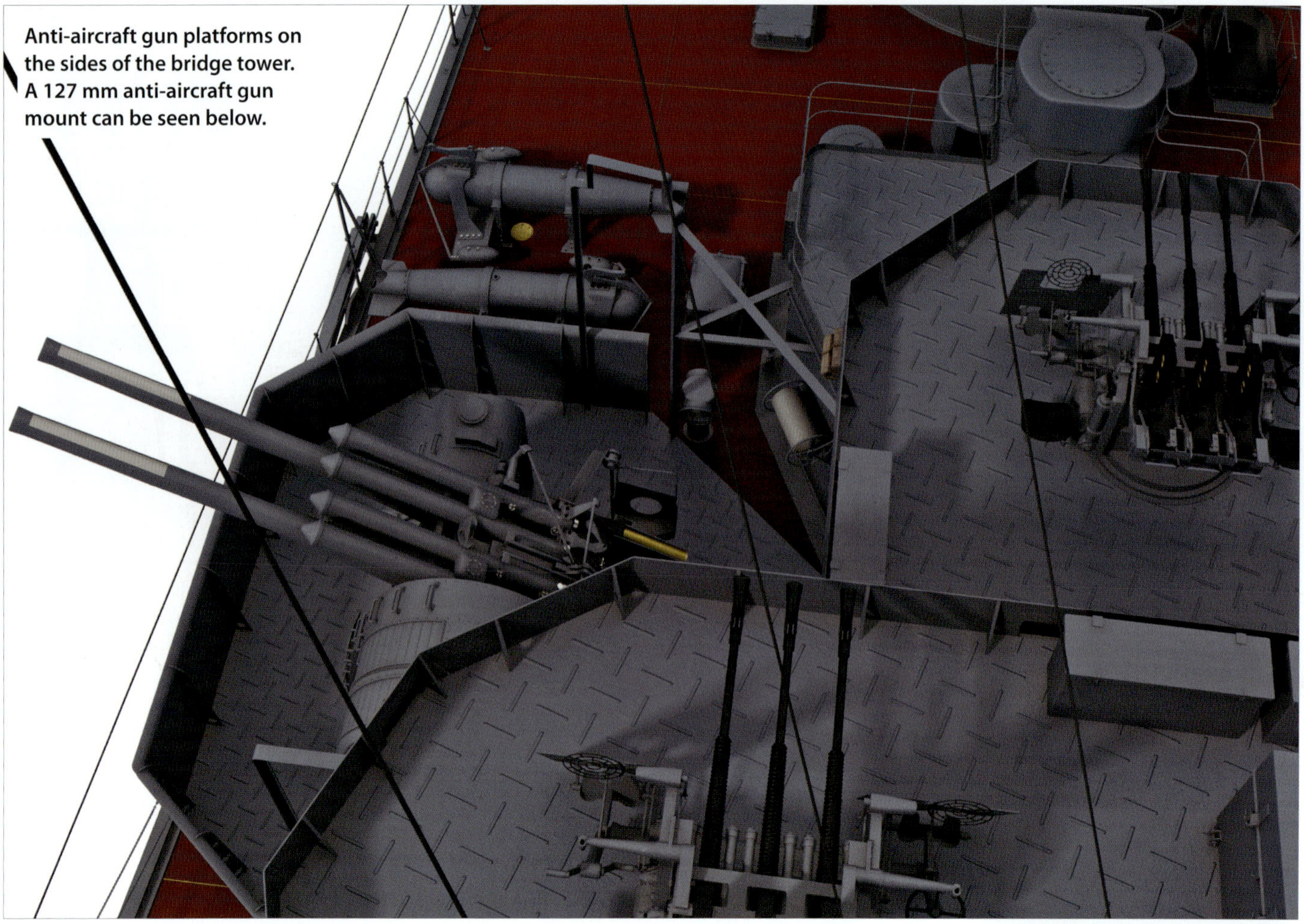
Anti-aircraft gun platforms on the sides of the bridge tower. A 127 mm anti-aircraft gun mount can be seen below.

Platform braces and support structure of the bridge tower.

Details on the port side of the bridge tower.

A port side view at the base of the bridge tower.

Air intake on the side of the bridge tower.

9 m cutter on radial davits.

Lattice base of the foremast.

Signalling flags storage.

Rear wall of the bridge tower.

Rear view of the foremast with Type 13 radar antenna visible.

The cruiser's funnels.

Anti-aircraft gun platforms amidship.

127 mm guns crew loading exercise machine.

Ship fittings in vicinity of the funnels.

127 mm anti-aircraft gun mount amidship.

Port side view of the midship.

Base of the mainmast on the aft superstructure.

Observation posts on the aft superstructure.

Port side view of the midship section. A catapult and the mainmast are visible.

Port side catapult and motor boats seen from atop the mainmast.

Port side catapult and the motor boats.

11.5 m motor boat seen from the boat deck level.

Fresh water tanks on the boat deck.

A passageway under the aircraft deck leading to the quarterdeck.

Details of the aircraft deck.

Floatplane deck transport trolley.

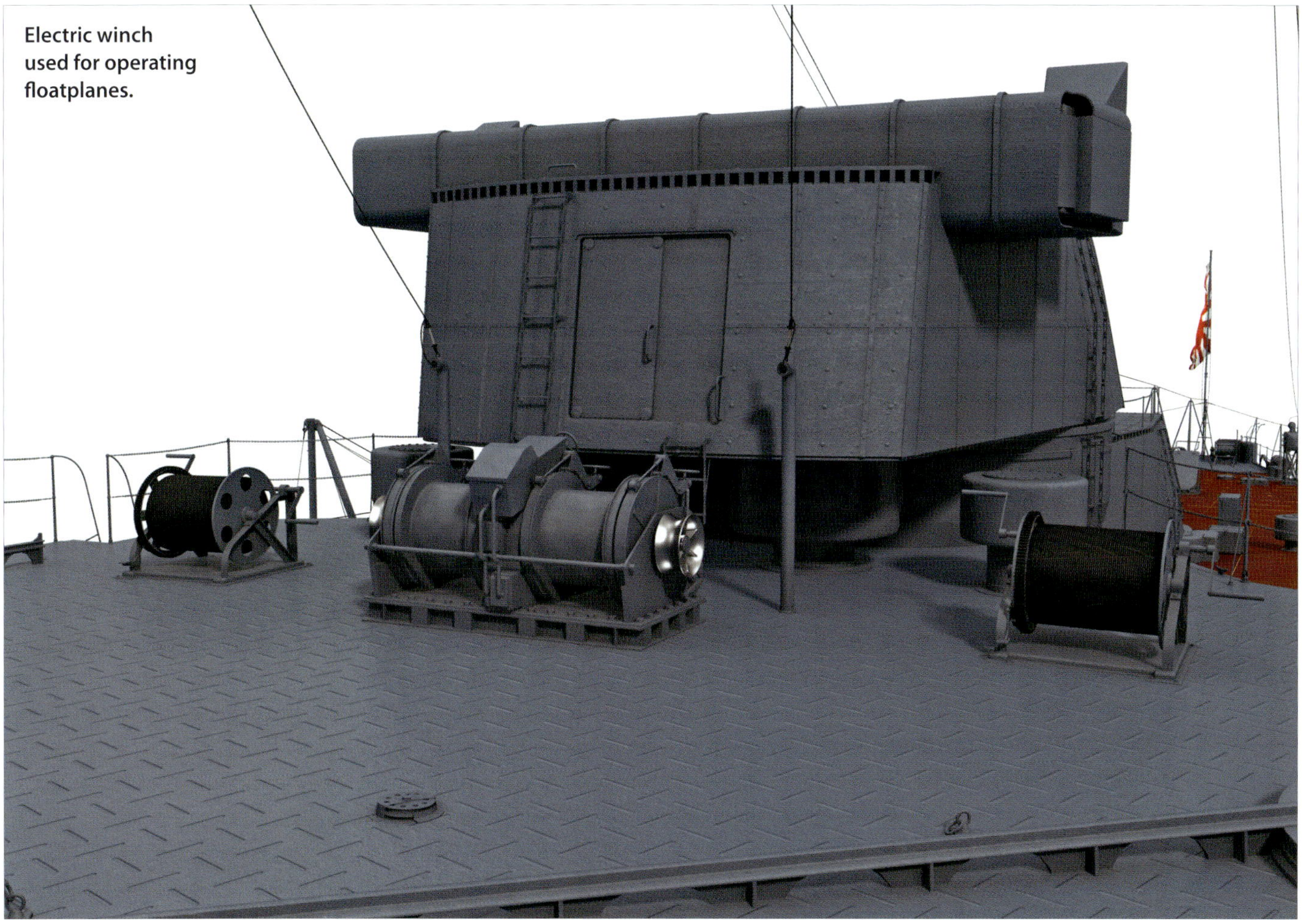
Electric winch used for operating floatplanes.

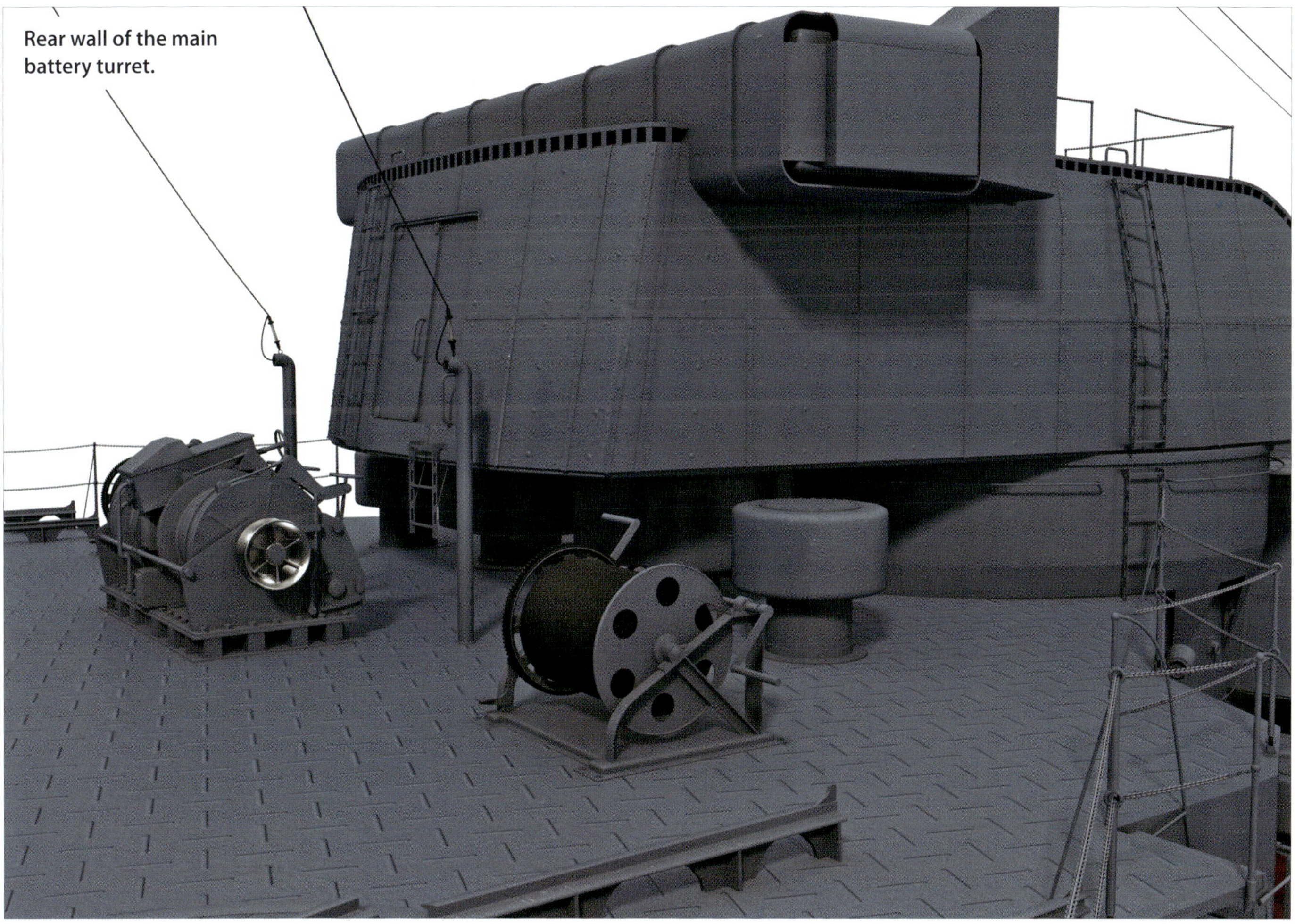
Rear wall of the main battery turret.

Main battery guns as seen from the aircraft deck.

A passageway leading from the aircraft deck to the quarterdeck.

A single 25 mm gun mount on the quarterdeck.

Swinging boom on the port side.

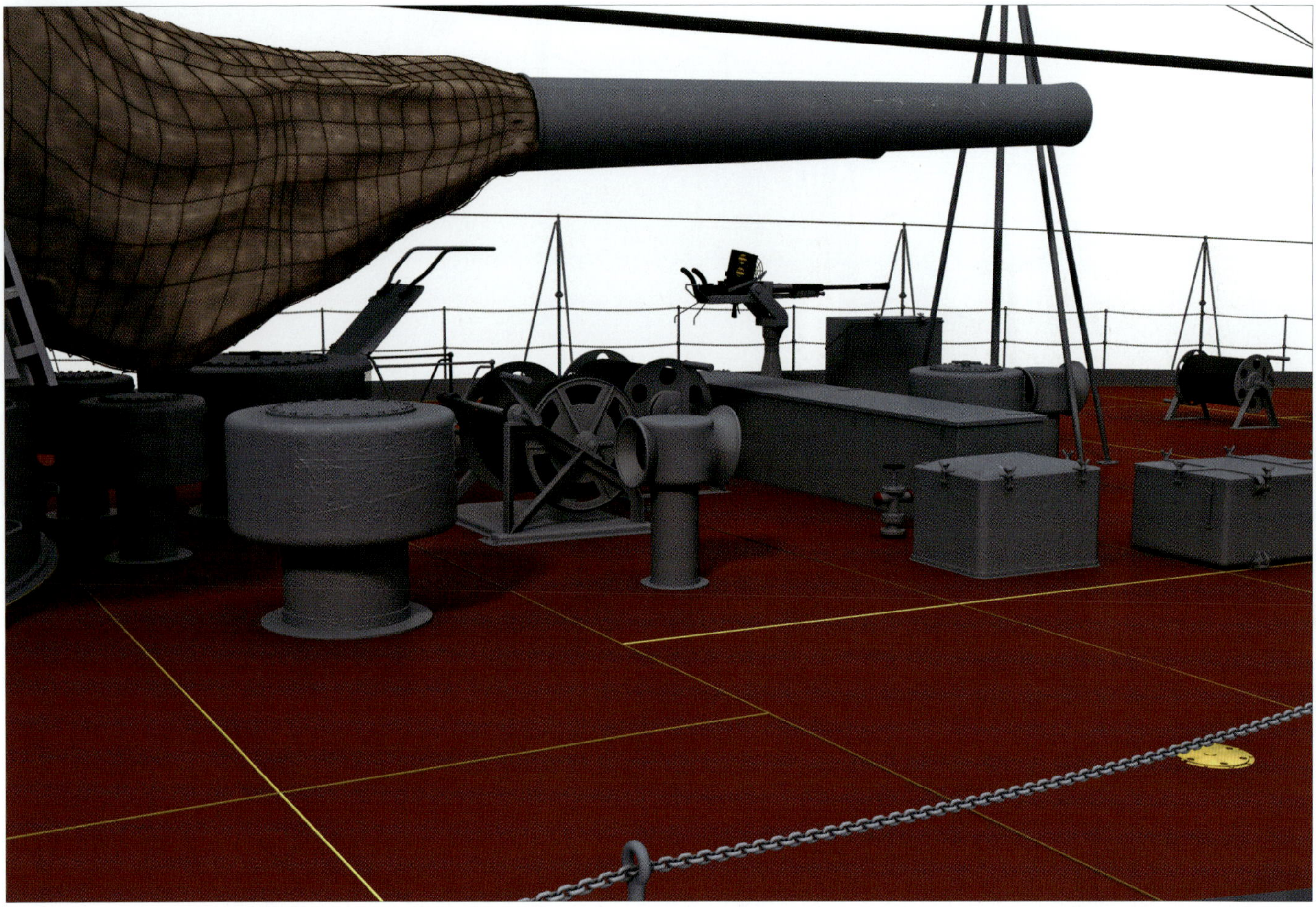

Fittings on the quarterdeck.

Stern main battery turrets.

Outer propeller folding limiter and inner propeller limiter.

Stern view. Japanese Imperial Navy ensign is flown from the flagstaff.

A view of the quarterdeck looking towards the stern.

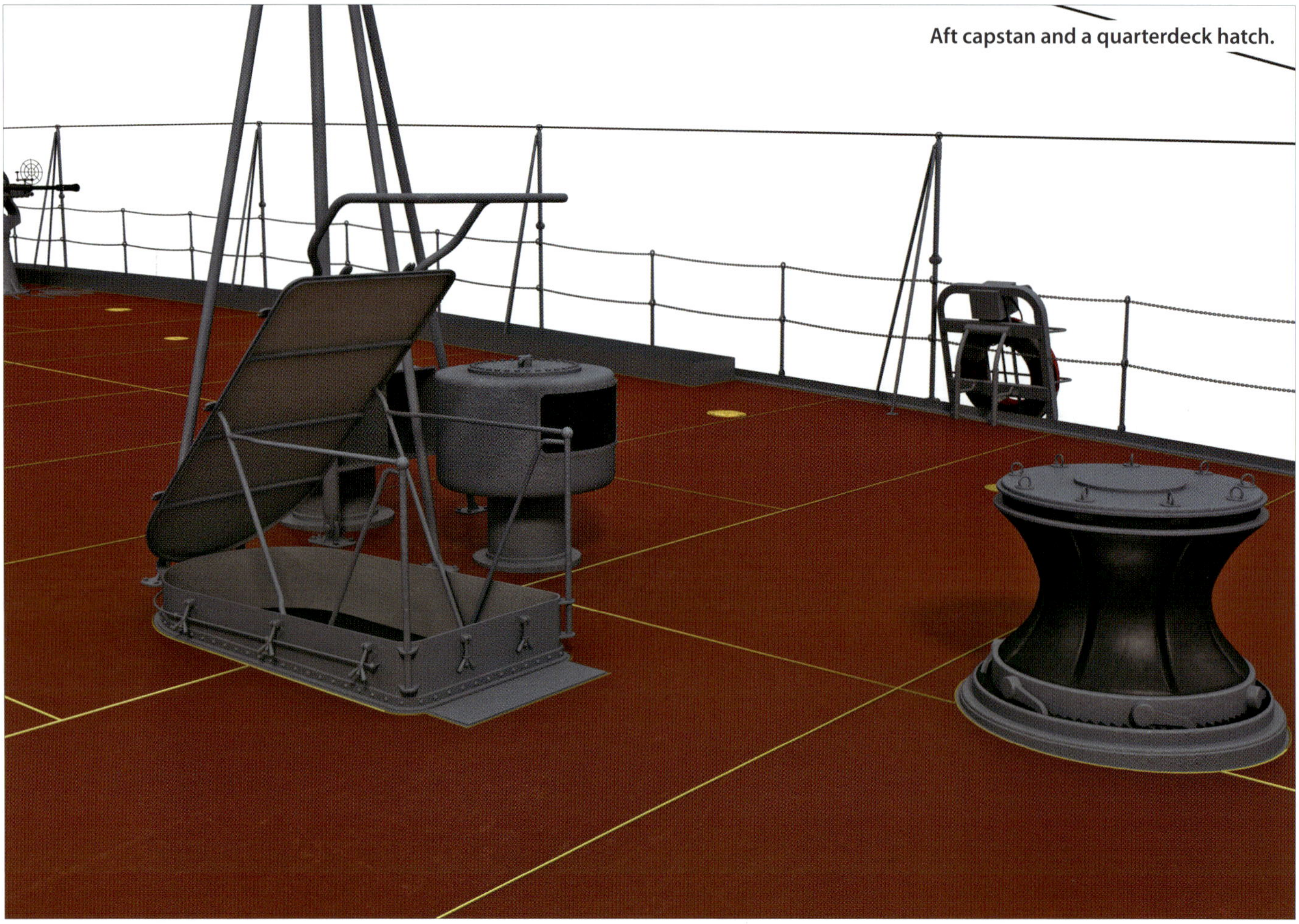

Aft capstan and a quarterdeck hatch.

A view from the quarterdeck looking towards the bow.

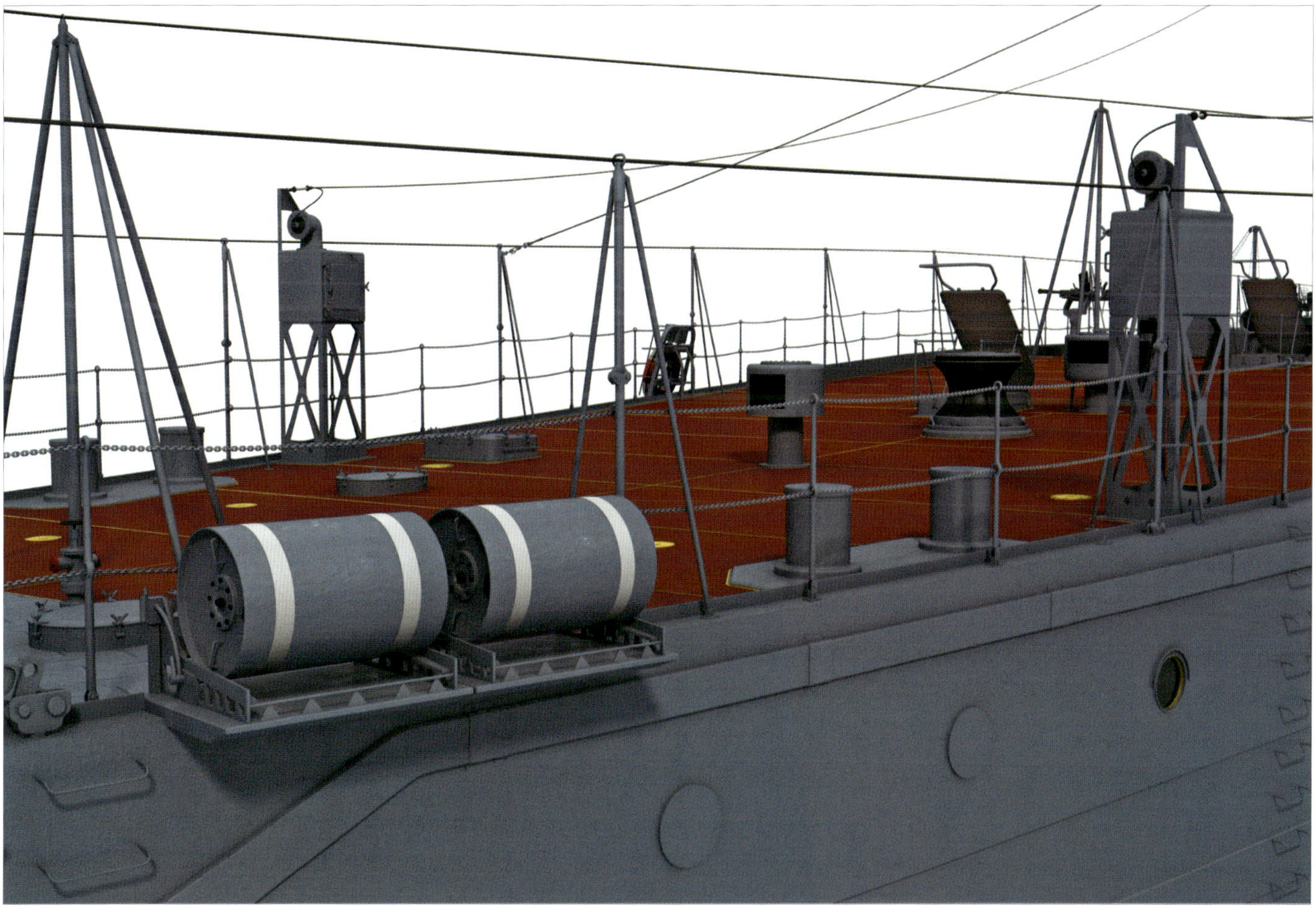

Depth charges chutes.

Depth charge chutes as seen from the quarterdeck.

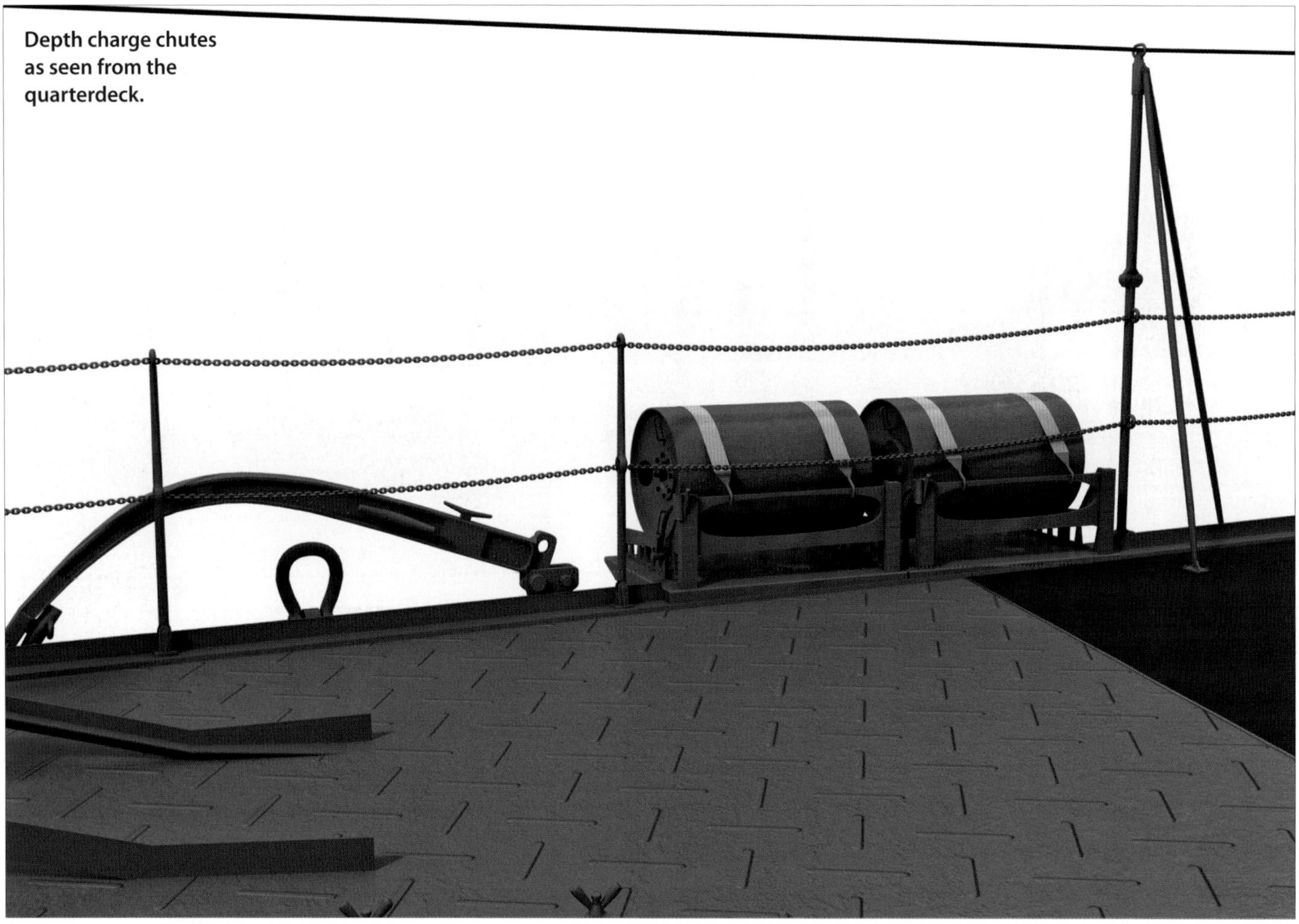

Depth charges rack at the stern.

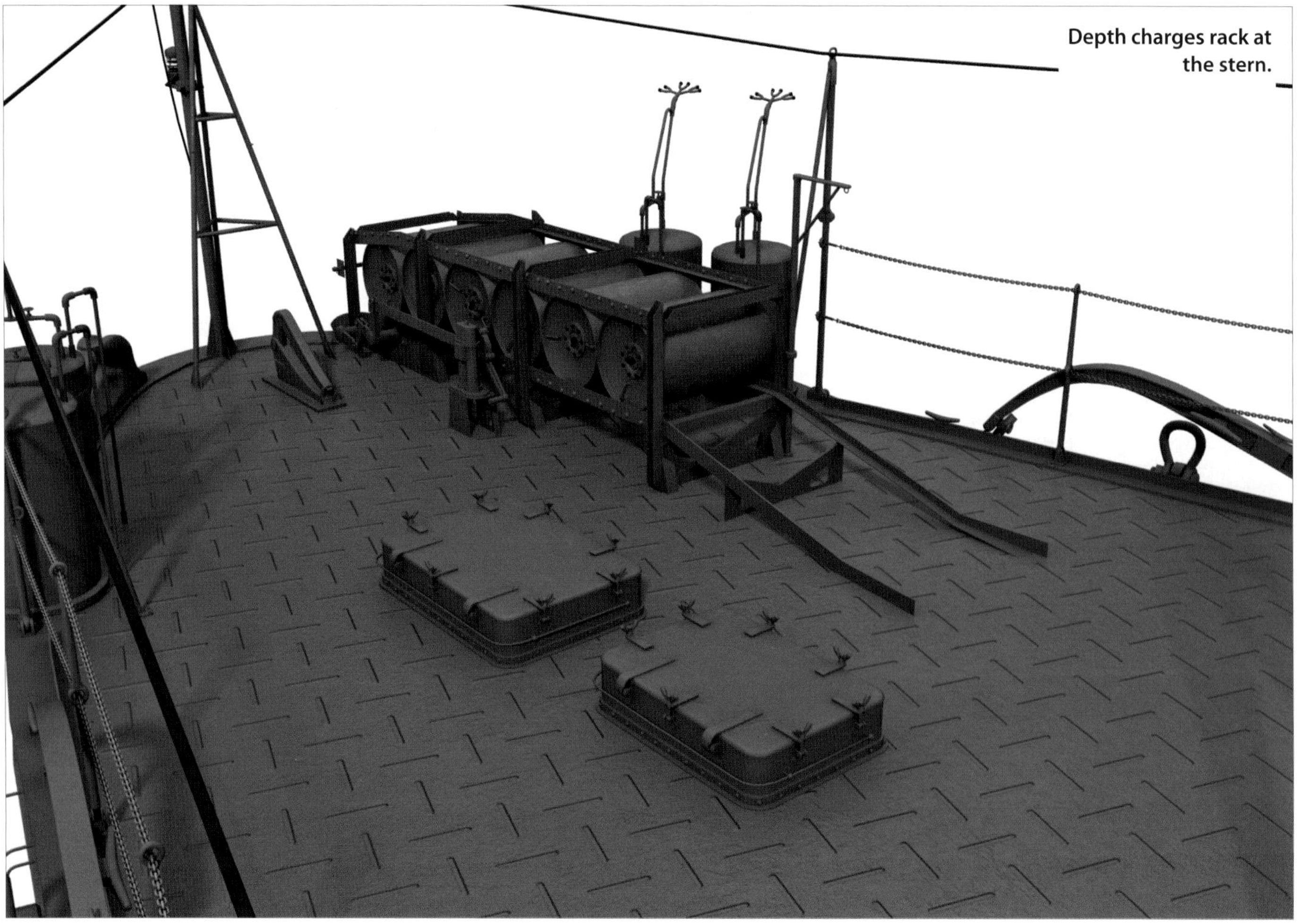

Stern anchor.

Smoke screen generator and depth charges rack.

Stern view of the cruiser *Maya*. Imperial Navy ensign can be seen in the foreground.

A view from the quarterdeck towards the stern.